The LEGACY *Life*

DEVOTIONAL

LIVING A LIFE THAT MATTERS FOR ETERNITY

DAVID GREEN
with Bill High

a division of Baker Publishing Group
Grand Rapids, Michigan

© 2025 by Hobby Lobby Stores, Inc. and Generational Legacy Counsel, LLC

Published by Baker Books
a division of Baker Publishing Group
Grand Rapids, Michigan
BakerBooks.com

Printed in China

All rights reserved. No part of this publication may be reproduced, stored in a retrieval system, or transmitted in any form or by any means—for example, electronic, photocopy, recording—without the prior written permission of the publisher. The only exception is brief quotations in printed reviews.

Library of Congress Cataloging-in-Publication Data
Names: Green, David, 1941 November 13– author. | High, Bill, author.
Title: The legacy life devotional : living a life that matters for eternity / David Green, Bill High.
Description: Grand Rapids, Michigan : Baker Books, a division of Baker Publishing Group, [2025] | Includes bibliographical references.
Identifiers: LCCN 2025000064 | ISBN 9781540904812 (cloth) | ISBN 9781493451135 (ebook)
Subjects: LCSH: Families—Prayers and devotions.
Classification: LCC BV255 .G635 2025 | DDC 249—dc23/eng/20250215
LC record available at https://lccn.loc.gov/2025000064

Unless otherwise indicated, Scripture quotations are from the Holy Bible, New International Version®, NIV®. Copyright © 1973, 1978, 1984, 2011 by Biblica, Inc.® Used by permission of Zondervan. All rights reserved worldwide. www.zondervan.com. The "NIV" and "New International Version" are trademarks registered in the United States Patent and Trademark Office by Biblica, Inc.®

Scripture quotations labeled ESV are from The Holy Bible, English Standard Version® (ESV®). Copyright © 2001 by Crossway, a publishing ministry of Good News Publishers. Used by permission. All rights reserved. ESV Text Edition: 2016

Scripture quotations labeled MSG are from *The Message*. Copyright © 1993, 2002, 2018 by Eugene H. Peterson. Used by permission of NavPress. All rights reserved. Represented by Tyndale House Publishers.

Scripture quotations labeled NKJV are from the New King James Version®. Copyright © 1982 by Thomas Nelson. Used by permission. All rights reserved.

Some names and identifying details have been changed to protect the privacy of individuals.

Cover design by Chris Gilbert, Studio Gearbox

The proprietors are represented by the literary agency of A Drop of Ink, LLC.

Baker Publishing Group publications use paper produced from sustainable forestry practices and postconsumer waste whenever possible.

25 26 27 28 29 30 31   7 6 5 4 3 2 1

Acknowledgments

This devotional would not be possible without the hard work of our agent, Tom Dean, and the great team at Baker Books. We want to thank our families and especially our spouses, Barbara Green and Brooke High, for being our greatest fans, always.

Introduction

This devotional is designed to be a companion to *The Legacy Life: Leading Your Family to Make a Difference for Eternity*. It can be used as a stand-alone devotional as well.

This devotional is organized into three parts. Part 1 is "The Legacy Perspective." The goal of part 1 is to encourage you to think more long-term about your life, your family, and your impact. We want you to think for generations—generations of impact.

Part 2 of this book is "The Legacy Practices." Here we'll give you some practical instruction in a devotional context.

Part 3 is focused on "The Legacy Adventure." In this section, we'll give you real-life examples of families living the Legacy Life.

Introduction

A few notes on how to read this book: We have capitalized *Legacy Life* throughout this book to help you recognize it as a new way of thinking and of doing life. We want to encourage you to be an active reader. Read the verse. Read the surrounding context of the verse as well. But have a pen or highlighter in hand. Highlight or underline key phrases or words. Jot your notes in the margins.

Be particularly focused on how you can be action oriented. Take time to reflect on the devotion and then write down those reflections and your plan of action. These practical steps will help you on your journey of living the Legacy Life.

PART 1
The LEGACY PERSPECTIVE

DAY 1

LEGACY IS WHAT YOU PUT *in* MOTION
Part I

He did what was right in the eyes of the LORD and followed completely the ways of his father David, not turning aside to the right or to the left.

2 Kings 22:2

We struggle with the definition of legacy. The phrase used most often is that *legacy is what you leave behind*.

There are many unfortunate associations with the idea of what you leave behind. In some cases, legacy is tied to the idea of wills, trusts, and estate planning. No one typically gets too excited about meeting with a lawyer. Worse still, I remember talking to a man who said rather flippantly, "After I die, it's all up to them to figure it out."*

But the idea that legacy is what you leave behind is tied to a worldview that this world matters the most. That's not a biblical worldview. We are citizens of heaven. We live for that future day when we'll stand in heaven, when we'll see our loved ones and the lives we touched and be in relationship with the eternal God forever and ever.

Instead of saying legacy is what you leave behind, I like to say:

> Legacy is what you put in motion.

We live for that future day in heaven. We don't live for these temporary few days that we walk upon this earth.

We see that in the Scriptures. King David lived an adventurous life—from shepherd boy to king's attendant, to warrior, to rebel refugee, to king, to outcast, to king again. But even with such a great life, David was described first and foremost as a man of integrity and a man after God's own heart. Accordingly, God made an astounding promise to David: "Your house and your

---

*Anytime we use a first person "I" in a story, it is David Green speaking.

kingdom will endure forever before me; your throne will be established forever" (2 Sam. 7:16).

Let me put it differently. We see David, particularly in the Psalms, pour out his heart before God. He knew God as refuge, warrior, defender, and friend. Because David lived such a life set on God, in pursuit of God, yearning for God—not perfectly, by any means—he set in motion a legacy of righteousness.

The last good king in Judah was Josiah, who came eighteen generations after David. It's a span of roughly three hundred years from David to Josiah. It is a remarkable thing three hundred years later to say that Josiah "did what was right in the eyes of the LORD and followed completely the ways of his father David, not turning aside to the right or to the left" (2 Kings 22:2).

Can you imagine someone saying that about your life? That three hundred years from now, someone will still be saying, "Wow, they were just like their great-great-great-great-great . . . grandfather David!" And, of course, we hope that the testimony is one of honor, integrity, and righteousness.

O Lord, help me to set in motion a legacy of righteousness for generations to come.

DAY 2

LEGACY IS WHAT YOU PUT *in* MOTION
Part II

In the fifty-second year of Azariah king of Judah, Pekah son of Remaliah became king of Israel in Samaria, and he reigned twenty years. He did evil in the eyes of the LORD. He did not turn away from the sins of Jeroboam son of Nebat, which he had caused Israel to commit.

2 Kings 15:27–28

Legacy is not what you leave behind. It's what you put in motion.

The story of Jeroboam, son of Nebat, is a strange one. He was a rising star in Solomon's kingdom. He was singled out for advancement by King Solomon himself. But Solomon's heart turned away from God. As a result, the prophet Ahijah predicted that

Solomon's kingdom would be split—two tribes would remain with Solomon's son Rehoboam and ten tribes would end up under the rule of Jeroboam.

The prophet also made an amazing promise: Jeroboam would have an enduring kingdom if he walked faithfully like David did. Think about it: King David was revered. To have an enduring kingdom like King David would be incredible.

Ultimately, Ahijah's prophecy proved true. The kingdom was split, and Jeroboam ended up with ten tribes who recognized him as king. But instead of following the way of David, Jeroboam took a drastic turn. Fearing he would lose his position and power, he set up golden calves in the towns of Bethel and Dan.

Instead of setting in motion a kingdom legacy—an enduring legacy like David's—Jeroboam set out to steal worship from God. He actively led the nation of Israel away from the Lord. His leadership was so appalling that Ahijah later made a harsh prophecy against Jeroboam's entire household:

> Because of this, I am going to bring disaster on the house of Jeroboam. I will cut off from Jeroboam every last male in Israel—slave or free. I will burn up the house of Jeroboam as one burns dung, until it is all

gone. Dogs will eat those belonging to Jeroboam who die in the city, and the birds will feed on those who die in the country. The LORD has spoken! (1 Kings 14:10–11)

One chapter later, the prophecy against Jeroboam's house is fulfilled: Baasha "killed Jeroboam's whole family. He did not leave Jeroboam anyone that breathed, but destroyed them all" (1 Kings 15:29).

Jeroboam's legacy stands in stark contrast to King David's. Indeed, in 2 Kings 15, as Pekah assumed the throne in Israel—seventeen kings and two hundred years after Jeroboam—he was described as following in the sins of Jeroboam.

O Lord, help me realize that power and position are not important compared to the legacy I set in motion by living a life of righteousness.

DAY 3

LEGACY IS MORE THAN MONEY

> A good person leaves an inheritance for their children's children.
>
> Proverbs 13:22

Legacy is more than money.

I've seen more than one father leave his children and grandchildren a financial inheritance and totally regret it. One of them told me his children weren't productive and, even worse, his grandchildren had never really obtained jobs. Some had even chosen paths of excess and addiction. It was a sad story.

On the other hand, I think of a man who attended one of our CEO gatherings. Most of his life had been spent in ministry. He'd traveled quite a lot but always made a point of being at home for long seasons. He invested directly in his children with storytelling and biblical teaching. Each of his six children still follow

Jesus today. Even better, each of them found a spouse and have raised an army of grandchildren who exhibit the same faith.

Who has the greater legacy? The one with the money or the one with the children who follow Jesus? Of course, the Scriptures reflect a similar pattern. When we think about the greatest legacy in the world, we must think of Jesus Christ. He never traveled internationally or even far from home. He never appeared on a big stage. He didn't have a big social media following. He didn't build a big business. He didn't accumulate any financial wealth. His earthly possessions were literally few in number. He never married. He never had children. He was wrongly accused, wrongly convicted, and died a gruesome death.

Yet His legacy stands alone. Human history is marked by His death and resurrection. I'm afraid that we tend to think of legacy all too often as the gifts we'll leave our children in our will or trust. Legacy is so much bigger and broader.

When the Scriptures say that a good man leaves an inheritance for his children's children, we must consider that the first inheritance a person leaves is a good name. A name of integrity and trust. A reputation of honor and truth. But the second inheritance is the biggest—it is the inheritance of values and virtues. Teach your kids the value of hard work, of keeping your word, of loving your neighbor, of digging deep into Scripture, of serving others.

With these two inheritances—a good name and values and virtues—comes a simple truth. If we focus on a good and godly inheritance, we impact generations of lives because they'll keep it going. And they'll do this whether they receive a financial inheritance or not.

O Lord, help me to focus on leaving a good inheritance to my children—an inheritance of a good name and values and virtues. Help me to impact the generations of people who will receive and multiply this kind of inheritance.

DAY 4

THE BEAUTIFUL CITY

> If only for this life we have hope in Christ, we are of all people most to be pitied.
>
> 1 Corinthians 15:19

I'm in that season of life where's there's more in the rearview mirror than there is in the windshield. Someone told me that we need to envision our lives at eighty—sitting in our rocking chair on the front porch and telling stories to our great-grandchildren. I've got a lot of great stories to tell.

Because of our company, I've been able to travel the world. We've stopped in some of the greatest countries in the world. From time to time, we've been able to take some incredible leisure trips. We've seen a lot of great sights—the pyramids, the Nile, crystal-blue seas, plunging waterfalls, ice-blue glaciers, and incredible deserts that seemed barren yet so full of life.

Sometimes when I have these moments of reflection, I'm reminded that I was once just a poor kid from Oklahoma running barefoot in the summer. But even with all these great sights and experiences, I realize the best is yet to come. And I just have to say, I don't think we have enough messages about our ultimate destination.

Heaven is described as a place where there is no more crying and no more pain. Just that thought alone is enough to lift my spirits. It's a place where we'll need no light because we'll have the light of the Father. We'll get to experience His presence on a daily basis. Even though I've had a great marriage, we won't need marriage because we'll be complete—we'll no longer have that sense of being alone. What an incredible thought for those who have ever felt alone.

In this place of the long tomorrow, the old order of things will have passed away. Consider that those streets are paved with gold. The city walls are not made of stone but of jasper, sapphire, agate, emerald, onyx, ruby, chrysolite, beryl, topaz, turquoise, jacinth, and amethyst (Rev. 21:19).

I imagine in my mind's eye these incredible reunions. Seeing my dad, whole and new and strong again. My mom, ever graceful, gowned with the beauty of heaven. My brothers and sisters—the group together again.

Perhaps most of all, I can imagine the singing, the worship, and the peace of that place. It feels good even now as I think about it.

O Lord, indeed, I'm reminded that we do not put our hope in the things of this life. It is not our cars, our homes, or our careers. If we hope solely in these things, we are to be most pitied. No indeed, Lord, stir in our hearts this longing for home, our heavenly home. Show us the beauty of our eternal dwelling place.

DAY 5

THE MEANINGFUL LIFE

"Meaningless! Meaningless!" says the Teacher. "Utterly meaningless! Everything is meaningless." What do people gain from all their labors at which they toil under the sun? Generations come and generations go.

Ecclesiastes 1:2–4

It is perhaps one of the saddest verses in all the Bible. The writer of Ecclesiastes declares: "Life is meaningless!" And not just meaningless, but "utterly meaningless!" And why is life so meaningless?

While some debate the authorship of Ecclesiastes, most agree that the writer was most likely King Solomon. Who is Solomon? He came from a great family—his father was the famed King David. Solomon ascended to the throne, and he lived in a great era of peace. There was little strife during his reign.

Money? Solomon had lots of it. The Bible reports that he received 666 talents of gold annually, or twenty-five tons. Fame? The queen of Sheba visited just to be in the presence of his wisdom. Family? He had seven hundred wives. Activity? He did it all—building houses, vineyards, water projects, gardens, parks, flocks, and herds. He boasts, "I became greater by far than anyone in Jerusalem before me" (Eccles. 2:9).

Yet with all of this, Solomon sadly despairs, "It is all meaningless."

I'm afraid there are many who might share that same thought. There are some still who run so fast in building their lives, their families, and their businesses that they don't take the time to contemplate the reason *why* they are running so hard. There are others who are running away—whether through pleasure, medication, or numbness—so they never take the time to confront that nagging feeling that there might be more.

But there's good news. Solomon doesn't end with the meaninglessness of life. Instead, by the end of Ecclesiastes, he points the way to a meaningful life—a Legacy Life. What's a Legacy Life? It's a life of meaning, value, significance. It's a life that matters. It's a life that lasts.

How do you get there? Solomon offers this challenge: "The words of the wise are like goads, their collected sayings like firmly embedded nails" (Eccles. 12:11). Goads are like spurs—they drive us along to a destination. Let's jump into the journey of the Legacy Life.

O Lord, I don't want the statement about my life to be that "all is meaningless!" I don't want to build, acquire, and run so hard that I never stop to consider what a meaningful life looks like. Help me to take instruction from Your Word about how to build a Legacy Life.

DAY 6

ETERNITY *in* OUR HEARTS

He has also set eternity in the human heart.

Ecclesiastes 3:11

He was one of nineteen children born to witchcraft-practicing parents. He was severely abused as a child. By the age of fifteen, his parents exiled him to New York to live with his brother. That didn't last long. He was recruited into a gang where all his rage and anger allowed him to rise to the top. The alcohol, the violence, and the women revolved in an endless cycle of meaninglessness. Nicky Cruz was running as fast as he could from a life with God.

He was arrested many times and was told that his life was hopeless. He was destined for an early death. His best friend died in his arms.

Nicky hated the nighttime. When all the wars had ceased, and he was alone and quiet, the nightmares came. They were like the relentless reminder of the voices he could not stop. They were the reminder that he was on a certain path to destruction. But they were also the beginnings of the whisper of God that there was something beyond this life.

A "skinny country preacher" named David Wilkerson brought a simple message of the love of Jesus Christ to the streets of New York, and as much as Nicky fought it, God's love broke through.[1] In the decades since he was saved, Nicky has shared the gospel with millions of at-risk youths. His story is dramatic, but it's also like a thousand other stories.

God's Word is true: He puts eternity in the human heart. We all have a longing that our lives would be safe, secure, and long-lasting—eternal. But whether we have a church background or not, we instinctively realize that our lives are not eternal. They are temporal.

Every day we are faced with the reality that we could exit this planet at any moment. A car accident. A cancer diagnosis. The trouble in our world reminds us that none of us can control the timing of our entry or our exit. We can exercise seven days a week, eat the very best food, and still die early. I'm reminded of Jim Fixx, the author of the bestselling book *The Complete Book of Running*. At the age of fifty-two, Fixx died while out running.

Our God is a God of order. He builds things to last—not for destruction. He wants our lives to last. He wants the impact of our lives to last for eternity. He wants our families to last and to continue for generations of eternal impact. That's why He puts eternity in the heart of His people. In our heart of hearts, we know that there's nothing in this world that can satisfy. Not fame. Not power. Not land. Not houses. Not great wealth. We all exit to the long tomorrow.

O Lord, thank You that You've put eternity in my heart. Thank You for reminding me that there's nothing in this world that can satisfy. Let me live as an alien and exile on this earth and as a citizen of heaven.

DAY 7

THE FIRST RECOGNITION

Life Is a Vapor

> Why, you do not even know what will happen tomorrow. What is your life? You are a mist that appears for a little while and then vanishes.
>
> James 4:14

The apostle James asks one of the most penetrating questions: What is your life?

I remember growing up in the 1940s, and unlike today, there weren't things like video games, computers, sporting events, and moms who worked to keep us busy. Instead, we were told to head outside and find something to do. But even with our creativity, there were still times when the days just seemed to crawl by. Life seemed long.

Then, in the early part of my career, life was fun and fast. It was thrilling to approach life and work with all the energy I could pour into things. Growing and building a business and a family always seemed to put the next challenge in front of me, and the runway seemed long.

Even as I matured (buzzword for growing older) and my children were graduating and establishing their own careers, life still seemed busy, full, and with so much to look forward to. I suspect that in the natural seasons of life, it's not until the grandchildren come that we start to look into the rearview mirror more.

But there was one day driving down the 101 in Phoenix when an oncoming car jumped the lane and hit our car nearly head-on. A matter of degrees and the outcome would have changed for us—all in just one second. That's how quickly life changes. How quickly it can go away.

Your life is a vapor.

James drives this point home: "You do not even know what will happen tomorrow" (4:14).

It's one of the first beginnings of the Legacy Life—to realize the shortness of life. We are not guaranteed tomorrow. We have *this* today.

The First Recognition

I see so many people who wait to live the life God called them to until they hit some kind of vague milestone. It's a "when, then" kind of life. "When the kids are out of diapers, then I'll spend more time praying." "When I get that promotion, then I'll start to give." "When I get my business established, then I'll spend more time at home." "When we get the house paid off, then we'll go on that vacation we've been planning." The wise person, the one who wants to lead the Legacy Life, recognizes the brief span of life.

O Lord, thank You for this today. Help me to be reminded that my life is a vapor, and that each day is a gift. And because of that recognition, help me choose to invest today in the things that matter.

DAY 8

THE LONG TOMORROW

> No longer will there be any curse. The throne of God and of the Lamb will be in the city, and his servants will serve him.
>
> Revelation 22:3

Some years ago, we built the house that we are living in now. To be honest, it was a lot of fun to build it. I got out on the land, cleared the brush, and burned the debris, and after a hard day of work, it was fun to see the progress. We spent a lot of time looking at plans, deciding on the right site, elevations, angles, and views. When the build began, there was an equal amount of time spent selecting materials, making adjustments, and choosing colors. After the build was done, it was almost anticlimactic to move in.

I spent a lot of time dreaming of and building a house I might live in for twenty to twenty-five years. I admit that I don't spend nearly enough time thinking about heaven, the place I'll live in for eternity.

My coauthor, Bill, tells the story of sitting down some years ago with a man who had built a great business. His sons, however, had bought him out, and by that time he was fully out of the business. When asked about that process, he said with a twinkle in his eye that he had cancer. He was not down and out at all about his cancer. When Bill asked him why, he said with that same look of mirth that he was "studying for the final exam."

Bill tells a similar story about his friend Steve. While walking across their college campus, Steve would occasionally stop and leap into the air. The "what in the world are you doing" look from his friends was answered by a joyful exclamation: "I'm preparing for the rapture and going to meet Jesus!"

I remember a similar discussion with a business owner named Todd. He'd had a fretful meeting with his attorney, and there seemed to be a thousand decisions around how to address taxes, estate taxes, and how much he should leave his children. There was little discussion, however, on how he might give more to the kingdom both now and in the future. After an uncomfortable pause, a trusted advisor asked him a probing question: "Todd, what are you doing to prepare for the long tomorrow?"

I love the wisdom of that line. We do so much work, so much scurrying around, so much fretting, and spend so much energy building houses that we will only live in for a very short today. I wonder if God watches all our anxious toil and calls out, ever gently, "O David, what are you doing to prepare for the long tomorrow?"

O Lord, thank You for this reminder from Your Word that heaven is going to be a wonderful place—a place where there will no longer be any curse. Help me to ready myself for the long tomorrow.

DAY 9

KEEP *the* SHORELINE *in* MIND

> The twelve gates were twelve pearls, each gate made of a single pearl. The great street of the city was of gold, as pure as transparent glass.
>
> Revelation 21:21

There's this story of the businessman who negotiated with God. He asked God for permission to take just one suitcase to heaven when he died. After much pleading, God relented. Delighted, the businessman packed a suitcase full of gold. Upon his death, the man lugged his suitcase along. At his arrival to heaven, he was greeted by angels who quizzed him about the suitcase. He gleefully opened it for them. The angels were puzzled and asked him, "Why did you bring pavement?"

While the story brings humor, I'm afraid that it illustrates our own misconceptions of heaven. Heaven will be more beautiful, more delightful, and more abundant than anything we can conceive. Jesus said it this way: "My Father's house has many rooms" (John 14:2). That word *rooms* is the Greek word *monai*, which can be translated as "mansions." Compared to the drab—at best, modest—homes of the Jewish villages, Jesus is expressing the wonder and grandeur of heaven's mansions.

Stephen Covey, in his bestselling book *The 7 Habits of Highly Effective People*, said it simply, "Begin with the end in mind."[1]

Florence Chadwick was a long-distance swimmer. She was the first woman to swim across the English Channel, a swim she ultimately completed four times in her career. In 1952, she attempted to complete a swim from Santa Catalina Island to the coast of California. She was accompanied by trail boats to ward off sharks and provide assistance if needed.

The weather was foggy and chilly. At times, she could hardly see the accompanying boats. She begged to be taken out of the water. Her mother, who was in one of the trail boats, encouraged her to keep going—she wasn't far! Fifteen hours into the swim, Florence was pulled into the boat.

Keep the Shoreline in Mind

When she looked up, she saw that she was just a half mile away from the shoreline. At the press conference, she was asked what went wrong. She said, "If I could have seen land I know I could have made it."[2]

Two months later, Florence attempted the same swim and completed it. What was the difference? She said that the entire time she kept the shoreline in mind. Her story challenges us to consider whether we are focused on pavement or heaven.

O Lord, I confess that I'm too often caught up in the material and miniscule pursuits of this world. Help me to always keep in mind that heaven is my shoreline!

DAY 10

THE GENERATIONAL LENS

> I will establish my covenant as an everlasting covenant between me and you and your descendants after you for the generations to come, to be your God and the God of your descendants after you.
>
> Genesis 17:7

I've been wearing glasses for a long time now. Without glasses, I can see distant objects and signs only with vagueness, blurriness, and dimness. I wouldn't know if the speed limit was 35 mph or 55 mph. But when I slip my glasses into place, it's amazing how what was fuzzy becomes sharp and defined.

It's the difference of a lens.

Perhaps you've seen the videos of children who get their first pair of glasses. Previously their world was cloudy and undefined. What's more amazing to me is that their body language seems to reflect that blasé, indistinct droopiness. But when those corrective lenses are slipped on, suddenly their world explodes with light, color, and precision, and that which was droopy lifts with the excitement of clear vision.

It's the difference of a lens.

In our present culture, we tend to look at our lives through the lens of individualism. It's about my life, my career, my family, my time, my achievements. The lens of individualism focuses on my life as the one-act play debuting for an audience of one—myself. Oftentimes, even the concepts of marriage and family are about the happiness and satisfaction they bring *me*.

But there's a different lens: a generational lens. When God was speaking to Abraham about His covenant, He told him that it would be an everlasting covenant. Everlasting. We don't use that word a lot today, but it's something that doesn't wear out.

I don't know about you, but the concept of an everlasting covenant with God sounds incredible. But God didn't stop there: The everlasting covenant was between Abraham and his descendants. God then went even further: The covenant was between Abraham, his descendants, and the generations to come.

God wanted Abraham to look beyond himself and his children. He wanted him to use a generational lens and look to the generations to come.

So let me encourage you to try on a new pair of eyeglasses. Can you look to your children, your grandchildren, your great-grandchildren, and the generations beyond them? Can you imagine a long line of descendants—an everlasting line—of people who would say that they know and worship God?

O Lord, change my lens from one focused on just myself and my children. Give me a generational lens—generations of those who still follow You!

DAY 11

OUR GOD IS a GENERATIONAL GOD

Part I

Then he said, "I am the God of your father, the God of Abraham, the God of Isaac and the God of Jacob."

Exodus 3:6

Who is God to you? Have you ever done a Bible study on the names of God? He has many. Jehovah Jireh—God is provider. Jehovah Rapha—God the healer. Jehovah Nissi—God my banner. Jehovah Shalom—God is peace. And, perhaps the most famous, Jehovah Rohi—God is my shepherd.

These names of God are most helpful when we think of God. But I think we often miss the generational character of God. Think about Moses. He grew up in the palace of Pharaoh. Life must've been good there.

Servants at every turn. The best food. The best education. A privileged life.

But Moses knew better. Before ever going to the palace, Moses knew his true identity. He was an Israelite. He knew they were God's chosen people. But still his perspective was too small. Even though his head knew who God was, his heart didn't really know God.

When he saw an Israelite being mistreated, Moses took matters into his own hands, and he murdered the Egyptian who committed the ill treatment. Moses seemed to think that he could single-handedly deliver Israel. But his view of God was too small. He seemed to think that God was too small to save them, that he was a far-off and distant god.

For his own misdeeds, Moses fled to the wilderness. I suspect that it was there in the wilderness that Moses truly went to school. There, in vast open spaces and under sprawling starry skies, with harsh winds, freezing nights, pelting rain, and sometimes nothing but silence, Moses slowly but surely began to understand.

Alone except for the sheep he was tending, Moses encountered a burning bush and turned to meet God. How did God introduce Himself? He said, "I am the God of your father, the God of Abraham, the God of Isaac, the God of Jacob" (Exod. 3:6). It's like this dramatic, zoom-out, 3D theater. He is a generational God.

The message is implicit and profound. God is far bigger than my life. He's bigger than any deliverance I can achieve on my own. Indeed, He's been the God of my father, my father's father, and all the generations before. In the same way, He's the God of the generations to come. He sees my children, my grandchildren, great-grandchildren, and beyond. He wants us to view Him the same way—as a generational God.

O Lord, I'm truly grateful that, like with Moses, You rescued me from a life of chaos, and You've chosen me as a citizen of Your kingdom. You remove my shame and call me royalty. But Your call is so much bigger than me. You are a generational God. You are the God of generations past and generations to come!

DAY 12

OUR GOD IS *a* GENERATIONAL GOD
Part II

Who has done this and carried it through, calling forth the generations from the beginning? I, the LORD— with the first of them and with the last—I am he.

Isaiah 41:4

I think Job got it right.

Because of the nature of my work—looking for the best products—I've been able to travel the world. Australia, New Zealand, Thailand, Vietnam, India, China, England, Greece—there are probably just a few countries that I've not been able to see.

Through those travels, I've been able to witness some incredible views. The crowded streets of Thailand. The raw beauty of New Zealand. Perhaps one of my favorites was traveling across Canada by rail and experiencing panoramic views of mountains and plains exploding in color. Personally, I've never grown tired of exploring the desert in and around Arizona. I love the stark beauty there.

Job said it this way: "And these are but the outer fringe of his works; how faint the whisper we hear of him! Who then can understand the thunder of his power?" (26:14). We see and understand so little of our Creator God. That's why it will take all of eternity to understand and worship Him.

In the same way, I think we limit God: we see Him as a God of *our* time. Our present moment. We pray for bread and sustenance for the day. We live, we work, we get married, we have babies, we watch them grow up, and we head to the gray-haired seasons of life.

Maybe there will be grandchildren, and perhaps even great-grandchildren. Perhaps we are given eighty years of life, and that is all we see.

But our God is so much bigger. He is so far beyond our eighty years. He is truly the everlasting God. He is the God of generations, which is why I love these words in Isaiah: "Calling forth the generations from the beginning? I, the LORD—with the first of them and with the last—I am he" (41:4). He calls out the generations. He thinks and plans generationally. He shapes the destiny of nations. He sees from Genesis to Revelation.

Our eighty years are but a shadow in how our God sees the world. It staggers me to think that God thought about all the generations of people that would lead to me and my little life. More than that, He has thought of every generation of humankind to orchestrate and shape the history of the world—past, present, and future. There is a grand and divine narrative that only He knows and understands.

He is a God of the generations. We worship Him for that.

O Lord, I stop to pause and wonder that You are the God who calls out the generations. You are the shaper of the destiny of humankind and of nations. It creates in me a sense of awe, and I worship You.

DAY 13

GOD THINKS *and* PLANS GENERATIONALLY

> Then the LORD said to him, "Know for certain that for four hundred years your descendants will be strangers in a country not their own and that they will be enslaved and mistreated there. But I will punish the nation they serve as slaves, and afterward they will come out with great possessions."
>
> Genesis 15:13–14

At Hobby Lobby, we've always tried to keep things pretty simple.

I know that there are companies and organizations that do lots of forecasts, market studies, and lots of strategic planning. I applaud them for that, and there are times when I might wish for more of that. But for us, we've tried to do two primary things: add stores in great locations and make our stores better for each and every customer. That's it.

Think about Abraham. He's really a lot like me and you. He was a pretty normal guy. He lived in Harran. He had a mom and dad. We don't really know much about them. He had aunts and uncles. There were probably lots of kids and cousins running around. Abraham got married, which was a big deal, to a girl named Sarah. Like a lot of people, he fixated on having a kid, a son in particular.

Then things got interesting. God asked him to move to a distant land, and He said He'd give him that land. But not immediately. In fact, all Abraham would get to be is a tourist in the land.

Perhaps to demonstrate that He was serious about His promise, God made a covenant—a contract—with Abraham. He told him that the land was Abraham's, but then He laid out His strategic plan. Abraham's descendants would spend four hundred years in a foreign land. In slavery. Mistreated. After four hundred years, God would punish the nation that enslaved them, and Abraham's people would be set free with great possessions.

Can you imagine a four-hundred-year strategic plan for your life? Here's what's crazy about that plan: God told Abraham that he was going to die in peace and see his ancestors. In other words, Abraham wasn't going to see any of it. God's plan, His four-hundred-year plan, was only beginning to unfold with the life of Abraham.

God put an incredible legacy in motion with the life of Abraham. I'm not sure about you, but I love that. I'm also challenged to think differently. Our God is a generational planner.

Somehow, it takes pressure off the present moment. My immediate challenge is to be faithful in the present and allow Him to work His generational plan.

O Lord, You call the generations, and I acknowledge that You have a generational plan for my life. I realize that I may not see the plan's fulfillment, but I trust in Your good plan.

DAY 14

THE RESPONSIBILITY *to* GENERATIONS

> So your descendants will know that I had the Israelites live in temporary shelters when I brought them out of Egypt. I am the LORD your God.
>
> Leviticus 23:43

That phrase is power-packed: *so your descendants will know.*

The verse refers to the Festival of Booths. During the festival, the people of Israel moved out of their homes and lived in booths or tents for seven days. Why? Living in tents served as a reminder that Israel lived in tents when they escaped from Egypt and made their way to the promised land.

The festival was to be repeated every single year. You can imagine the upheaval caused by such a move—going from being surrounded by the comforts of home and then being forced to move to a booth or tent. It would take a lot of figuring out—what to bring, what meals to make, what you could do without. For the little kids, it was probably great fun. And memorable.

I remember hearing the story of a man in Japan. He walked to work every day, and every day he passed by a field where a farmer was clearing rocks from the field. The farmer picked, he dug, and then he carried the rocks to the side of the field. Every day, every season, the routine was the same.

Finally, the man grew curious. Why did the farmer never plant a crop? Why did he only carry rocks to the side of the field? One day, he stopped the farmer in the middle of his work. He repeated his thoughts: "Every day, I walk to work, and I walk by this field. Every day, I see you do the same thing. You pick, you dig, and you carry rocks to the side of the field. Why do you never plant a crop?"

The farmer smiled patiently and responded, "I'm preparing this field for my grandchildren."

This generational mindset stands in stark contrast to our world of immediate gratification. It changes the question of "What can I get out of this?" to "What will the future generations get out of this?" This generational mindset takes cultivation. After all, who thinks like that in today's world?

On the other hand, think about it. How would your attitudes, actions, and behaviors change if you knew that your grandchildren and your great-grandchildren were going to benefit? For myself, I know that as our company grew, I began to feel the weight of the generations. My early goals in life were to have a great marriage, a great career, and children who served the Lord. But I've since added prayers for my grandchildren and great-grandchildren to serve the Lord as well.

O Lord, thank You that Your Word gives us instructions to set up booths and to hold festivals as reminders to the generations that we are a people called to You. May we all have a generational mindset.

DAY 15

THE IMPACT *of* GENERATIONS

For Ezra had devoted himself to the study and observance of the Law of the LORD, and to teaching its decrees and laws in Israel.

Ezra 7:10

It's a powerful verse. Ezra devoted himself to study, to obey, and to teach God's law. Study, obey, and teach.

I've heard this verse quoted and taught many times. The verse demonstrates the diligence of Ezra. But I've got a question:

What made it possible for Ezra to do those things?

The Scriptures give us a powerful clue. Ezra 7:1–5 lists the genealogy of Ezra. There are a bunch of hard names to pronounce. But it goes like this: Aaron, the first priest, fathered Eleazar. Eleazar fathered Phinehas, who fathered Abishua, who fathered Bukki, who fathered Uzzi, who fathered Zerahiah, who fathered Meraioth, who fathered Azariah, who fathered Amariah, who fathered Ahitub, who fathered Zadok, who fathered Shallum, who fathered Hilkiah, who fathered Azariah, who fathered Seraiah, who fathered Ezra.

The truth is that most of us skip over the genealogies. They don't mean anything to us.

Here, the genealogy speaks powerfully. Aaron's role as the first priest speaks for itself, but his grandson Phinehas also made a big mark. At a time when Israel was drifting away from God through marriages to foreign women, he took a bold stand and slayed two brazen offenders. In recognizing his zeal to defend the purity of God's name, the Lord made a promise: "He and his descendants will have a covenant of a lasting priesthood, because he was zealous for the honor of his God" (Num. 25:13).

A lasting priesthood! After Eli's sons failed as judges in Israel, God spoke to Eli and said, "I will raise up for myself a faithful priest, who will do according to what is in my heart and mind" (1 Sam. 2:35). Many believe that prophecy was fulfilled first in Samuel, then Zadok, and ultimately Christ.

What's the point of this discussion of lineage? Ezra did not wake up one day and become a self-made man.

The Impact of Generations

Ezra 7:10—study, obey, and teach—doesn't happen in a vacuum. Ezra is part of the story, part of the lineage. I'm afraid that in our highly individualistic world we are inclined to only see Ezra without seeing that there was a bigger, broader, and ongoing narrative of what God was doing.

When we see that we are just part of the story, then we see the impact of generations before us, and the generations to come.

O Lord, I recognize that my view is too narrow. I tend to see only my story, my achievements, my family. Help me to realize the impact of those who have come before me and those who will come after me.

DAY 16

HIS MERCY IS *for* GENERATIONS

His mercy extends to those who fear him, from generation to generation.

Luke 1:50

My mom's dad was a preacher. She followed in his footsteps. He let her preach in those old-fashioned tent revivals. I know the idea of a woman preaching can be a hot-button topic, but I'm grateful she did. You see, it was at one of those tent revivals that my dad gave his life to Christ.

He was so touched by the message that he gave his life to the ministry. Together, he and Mom forged both a ministry life and what proved to be a Legacy Life. The churches they pastored in were generally small congregations, with a hundred people or fewer. The denomination we were in required pastors to move every two years, so no sooner would they get settled in a congregation than it was time to move again.

I can only imagine how hard it was for them to uproot themselves and their children from friends they'd only just made. The tears they might've shed were hidden from us. And I know it was tough to make ends meet. A family of six kids and two adults took some providing for.

To this day, I can still remember seeing them on their knees, crying out in prayer for God's provision, for God's blessing upon our family. In those days, I felt the angst of their prayers and the need. With the benefit of eighty-plus years now, I think I get a bird's-eye view of God's pleasure. I know God heard their prayers, and I suspect that He was most pleased by their resolute faithfulness. There was no turning back.

But I also believe that my parents had no idea what they had set in motion. All their children loved and served God. They either served as pastors or pastors' wives. Those children gave birth to a next generation who also loved and served God. I look now at my own little family where we are in the fourth generation of Christ followers. What a blessing!

My mother died in her late sixties, well before Hobby Lobby was anything close to the size it is today. She had no idea that our company would be able to give so generously, and to impact so many lives for the sake of the gospel around the world. She had no idea of the countless people who would have a Bible in their own language because of the ministry we get to do.

But I firmly believe that because my mom and dad were faithful with a little, God extended His mercy four generations more.

O Lord, help me to live a Legacy Life by being faithful today with what You've given me. Give me resolute faithfulness. And may Your mercy extend upon my life and my family for generations.

DAY 17

WE THINK TOO SMALL

When I consider your heavens, the work of your fingers, the moon and the stars, which you have set in place, what is mankind that you are mindful of them, human beings that you care for them?

Psalm 8:3–4

When I was seventeen or eighteen, I was still in high school and working at the local five and dime called McLellan's. I remember a manager there took a liking to me. He was one of the first people to put a dream inside of me. He told me I could be a store manager. I remember thinking at that time that would be a big deal.

Well, I did become a store manager, and later a district manager and a regional manager. It was while I was serving at one of the largest TG&Y stores in the country that God gave me a different dream.

We had a café inside our store. I was sitting with two other managers having a cup of coffee. One of the other managers, Larry Pico, suggested that we ought to go into business for ourselves. (Starting a business wasn't even my idea.) We all agreed.

We began investigating the idea and determined we could buy a woodchopper for $450 and $150 of moldings to begin making frames. We went out and pursued a loan from the bank. Larry and I signed up, but our third guy decided he didn't want the risk. He never signed up. Sometimes I wonder how he feels all these years later.

Even as I write these words, I know that God often thinks the same of us. We think too small. I was just hoping to graduate from high school. I was just hoping to become a store manager. At the beginning of my marriage, I was just hoping to raise three godly kids. At the beginning of our business, I was just hoping to survive.

But our God thinks so much bigger. He saw Hobby Lobby while I was thinking about just being a store manager. He saw thousands of people getting great jobs and thousands of people receiving the gospel when I was worrying about a loan for a chopper. He saw two more generations of children even after my own children.

Where are you thinking too small? He wants to use your life to impact the world for generations to come. That's in your work. The people you interact with. Your spouse. Your family. Dream about the generations to come. Can you picture them and call them to mind? God sees it!

O Lord, I love the fact that You see beyond me to the generations to come. Would You give me a vision for that kind of life? Help me not to think too small. You are a generational God, and I praise You.

DAY 18

WE SHOULD THINK *and* PLAN *for* GENERATIONS

> But the plans of the LORD stand firm forever, the purposes of his heart through all generations.
>
> Psalm 33:11

As I mentioned a couple devotionals back, my dad was a pastor when I was growing up, and in our denomination, pastors were typically transferred every two years. I sometimes joke that the denomination must've figured that a pastor only had two years' worth of sermons before he ran out.

As a result of all that moving around, I attended seven or eight schools during my childhood. It never felt like we had time to establish roots in any one community. In today's world, it seems much the same. Whether because of job transfers or kids graduating from college or just desiring a move to someplace fun, we don't see a lot of continuity. We often don't get to see what we've planted grow up.

Motivational speaker and teacher Dennis Swanberg tells the story of his great-grandfather who came from Sweden in the 1880s. He moved to just east of Austin, Texas. He built a house and planted shade trees—because in Texas you need some trees to break the wind and provide relief from the heat. When Swanberg's grandfather was just five years old, his great-grandfather passed away.

Swanberg recounts that his great-grandfather never got to sit under the shade trees that he planted. But his grandfather did, his mother did, and Swanberg and his two boys did. They've all sat under those oak trees, which have provided shade for generations. I love that story.

How do you plant a shade tree that will last for generations? It's the kind of life that we live. A life governed by a set of principles. My life verse, the principle that guides my life, is 1 Timothy 2:7: "This and this only has been my appointed work: getting this news to those who have never heard of God, and explaining how it works by simple faith and plain truth" (MSG). And as we establish these principles, we tirelessly repeat them.

I hope my future generations will always remember my love for the gospel and evangelism.

The Legacy Life plans for the generations—whether through principles or practices. Some of those practices may include a focus on the homestead, the family picture that gets passed down, or other heirlooms like the family watch, the family ring, the family table, or the wedding dress. But it is also having a clear vision for the future and creating opportunity for future generations. Perhaps it is future generations of entrepreneurs or pastors or missionaries.

Can you look ahead and see your great-grandchildren, your great-great-grandchildren? Can you think about planting a shade tree that will last for generations?

O Lord, help me think differently about my future generations. Help me see beyond my children and grandchildren. Help me plan for generations to come—to plant shade trees for generations.

DAY 19

GOD MAKES GENERATIONAL PROMISES

> I will establish my covenant as an everlasting covenant between me and you and your descendants after you for the generations to come, to be your God and the God of your descendants after you.
>
> Genesis 17:7

Once a year our family gathers for a family celebration. It's a time when we come together and remind ourselves of God's blessing upon our family. We also take the time to renew our family vision, mission, and values.

For Barbara and me, now in our early eighties, it makes us misty-eyed to see four generations in the same room. Our children, our grandchildren, and their children. It's a wild, noisy, busy time—wonderful! Perhaps

I'll live long enough and get to see one more generation born.

The promise that God made to Abraham boggles my mind. Essentially, God says, "I'm going to make a covenant between me and you, your descendants, *and for the generations to come.*" In fact, as you see the story play itself out in the Bible, you see that promise demonstrated time and time again.

While there's little doubt that Israel had its struggles, the Scriptures are filled with this ongoing theme of blessing. The gift of the promised land. The deliverance from Egypt. Battles won against incredible odds. A king like David who established a standard for the pursuit of God. Great prophets who brought God's Word and warning. It's an incredible love story of God's relentless pursuit of our wayward hearts.

But these generational promises are not just for Abraham. God made generational promises to others in Scripture, including David (an enduring kingdom), which He repeated to Solomon and offered to Jeroboam (although he turned it down). For example, in 2 Kings 10:30, God made a generational promise to Jehu: "Because you have done well in accomplishing what is right in my eyes . . . your descendants will sit on the throne of Israel to the fourth generation."

Exodus 20:5–6 offers us a look at the generational mindset of God: "I, the LORD your God, am a jealous God, punishing the children for the sin of the parents to the third and fourth generation of those who hate me, but showing love to a thousand generations of those who love me and keep my commandments." It is such a powerful contrast. While disobedience can affect the third and fourth generations, God's desire for blessing is to a thousand generations!

When I see my little group of four generations, I realize that God is just getting started.

O Lord, I realize that I think too small. You make Your promise of blessing to the generations—even to a thousand generations. May I live then as one fully under Your grace and fully responsive to Your call in my life.

DAY 20

GOD MAY FULFILL HIS PROMISES *in* GENERATIONS

All these people were still living by faith when they died. They did not receive the things promised; they only saw them and welcomed them from a distance, admitting that they were foreigners and strangers on earth.

Hebrews 11:13

We live in a microwave culture. We want to put our dinner in the microwave and have it come out perfect and complete in two to three minutes. I've always said that the worst thing that can happen is for a customer to walk into Hobby Lobby and expect to buy something and for us to not have it in stock. I don't want to order a hamburger and get it three days later. People want things now!

Hebrews 11 is sometimes called the Hall of Faith. It's like taking a tour of the great heroes of faith: Noah, Abraham, Isaac, Jacob, Joseph, Moses, Gideon, Samson, Samuel, David, and the prophets.

In the Old Testament, there's a powerful image of the promised land. God promised Abraham, "To your descendants I give this land" (Gen. 15:18). But Abraham didn't get it. Neither did his son Isaac. Or Isaac's son Jacob. Or any of Jacob's twelve sons, including Joseph. Even Moses, although he got to see the promised land—a land flowing with milk and honey—didn't get to go in and possess it. It wasn't until the time of Joshua that the promise of possessing the land was actually fulfilled.

Here's the simple truth: Our God is an everlasting God. He makes plans and promises that are sometimes not fulfilled for generations to come.

That thought challenges my patience. My microwave mindset. But it challenges me in a deep and personal way. Am I willing to invest *today* in a life of faithfulness, in a life of living in righteousness, knowing that the harvest may not come for generations?

That's the remarkable thing about Hebrews 11. Noah built an ark when there was no rain. Abraham set out not knowing where he was going. Abraham was willing to sacrifice his son, not knowing how God's promise would be fulfilled. Isaac and Jacob blessed their sons, trusting God to see those blessings through. Joseph asked that his bones be carried out for burial in the promised land. Time and time again, the people of God acted upon the promise of God, even though they had not seen it.

What was their secret? "They saw [the things promised] and welcomed them from a distance" (Heb. 11:13).

O Lord, I pray that You'll give me a generational mindset to Your promises. Help me to understand that, while Your promises may not be fulfilled for generations to come, what I do today matters. My conduct, my faith, all matter for future generations. My life impacts the generations.

DAY 21

GOD IS *the* OWNER

For the world is mine, and all that is in it.
Psalm 50:12

I was born in 1941. In those days, America had not reached its zenith. It was an up-and-coming superpower, but it wasn't until after World War II that America fully ascended to a place of dominance. As a kid growing up in the 1940s, the expectation was that you'd take a job, work most of your life, and, if you were lucky, you might have a few years of a slower pace. But the concept of retirement was by no means rooted in our culture.

That mindset of work permeated our lives. It was a big deal when I was able to buy my car. There was no such thing as getting help from my parents. It was up to me. The same thing was true when Barbara and I bought our first house. We worked, we saved, and then finally we were the proud holders of a new mortgage.

When we started our business, we took a calculated risk. We got a $600 loan to buy a chopper that could cut wood moldings. We glued the moldings together to make picture frames that we shipped out to different craft stores within our region. Eventually, we were able to lease six hundred square feet of retail space, which was really nothing more than an old house. As we grew, we eventually needed our own warehouse and distribution space. It seemed a miracle when we could purchase our first space.

Why do I spend so much time giving you the history of our little wins along the way? It's because the seeds of ownership were being planted at every turn. My car. My house. My furniture. My business. My success.

You've seen this movie. You've got two little children, and they each have perfectly good toys that they are playing with. Then one spies the toy held by the other child. Soon there's a tug-of-war going on with a single battle cry: "It's mine!"

We do that in our own lives. It's the subtlest of diseases. I'm the owner. It's mine. Maybe we don't go around putting labels with our name on them on everything in our house. But instead, it's as if we survey our world and take stock of our holdings—our house, our cars, our stock portfolio—and we take comfort in what we own.

But God says just the opposite. He says, "The world is mine, and all that is in it" (Ps. 50:12). God is the owner.

One of the keys to the Legacy Life is to recognize that God is the rightful owner of everything that you have. When we recognize His ownership of everything in our hands, we take a key step toward the Legacy Life.

O Lord, in this day and moment, I take this time to recognize that You are the owner of everything that I have. I acknowledge Your ownership. Thank You, Lord.

DAY 22

WHAT IS ALL THIS STUFF?

What do you have that you did not receive?
1 Corinthians 4:7

In the last devotional, we talked about how one of the keys to living the Legacy Life is the great recognition that God is the owner of everything. Understanding that great truth changes things dramatically.

One of the first great questions that flows out of that is: What do I own? The answer is nothing, nada, zip, zilch. Everything that I have goes back into the box at the end of the game. There's nothing that I take from this life. Solomon recognized this futility of life: "All come from dust, and to dust all return" (Eccles. 3:20).

Time and time again in Scripture, God repeats this thought. In Romans 9:20, Paul says, "Shall what is formed say to the one who formed it, 'Why did you make me like this?'" Jeremiah 10:14 says pointedly of

What Is All This Stuff?

the goldsmith, "The images he makes are a fraud; they have no breath in them." In Job 38, God gave Job a dressing-down and asked him these timeless questions: Where were you at the beginning of creation? Who made the stars? Who holds the seas in check? Who sets the sun on its course?

In the book of Corinthians, Paul addressed a growing divide in the church. What was the source of the divide? Some leaders had arisen who had grown proud of their own teaching and authority, in effect saying, "Look at me! Follow me!" Paul cut that off at the knees by asking a sobering question: "What do you have that you did not receive?" (1 Cor. 4:7). We can all stand to ask that question of ourselves.

Think about it. My salvation? It came from Him. My faith? It came from Him. My time, my country, and place of birth? It came from Him. When I look around my own little world, I can look at my cars, my house, my business, the warehouses, the stores, the people who work there, and I can take credit for nothing. It all came from Him.

There was a period in my life when I started to think I was pretty good. I had the Midas touch in business. Every store, every division, every region—they all prospered under my leadership. When we started Hobby

Lobby, it grew steadily, and by the time we got to twelve or thirteen stores, I was starting to look around my little kingdom and think, "Look what I've made!" But God humbled me and took my little kingdom to the verge of bankruptcy. He showed me He could take it all in a minute.

What do I have that I have not received?

O Lord, You are indeed the owner of everything. Everything that I have comes from You. Life and breath. Sunrise and sunset. Every new day comes from You. My family, my friends, my time, and my place on this earth are all a divine orchestration from You. I'm humbled and I'm grateful.

DAY 23

I'M *a* STEWARD

It is required of stewards that they be found faithful.
1 Corinthians 4:2 ESV

The Legacy Life starts with these understandings: God is the owner of everything. There's nothing that I have that did not come from Him.

So with that, a few fundamental questions arise: Who am I? What is my role? What am I supposed to do with what I've been given?

I'm a steward. I'm a steward of what God has put in my hand.

The word *stewardship* has taken on some strange meanings. It's gotten associated with capital campaigns. It's gotten associated with giving. It's even gotten associated with estate planning. But the definition is so much simpler.

If we go all the way back to the garden of Eden when God created Adam, we get a picture of this word.

To lay the groundwork, Adam didn't ask to be born. God was the Creator. He made everything, including the garden. And He placed Adam right in the center of the garden. He trusted Adam to take care of the place and gave him a simple mandate to be fruitful and multiply. Make the garden more beautiful and make it creative.

That's the essence of stewardship. It's a relationship of trust. God trusts us. He entrusts resources to our hands. And with that trust, He expects us to use those resources for His benefit. To make the world more beautiful and more creative. To draw more attention to Him and His goodness.

I remember the story I heard some time ago of a family who was seeking God. They'd reached a point in their lives where they'd worked hard, and they sensed that God was asking something of them. But they were confused. Was it to go to the mission field? Was it to give more? Was it to serve more? As they prayed, they asked for the Lord to speak. His message came in the form of a question: "What have I put in your hand?"

What a great question! What has God put in your hand? What resources? What talents, abilities, time, people? Use them for His sake. Use them for His glory.

Seek to multiply and make the garden around you more beautiful and more creative.

That's the role of a steward.

O Lord, thank You for gently loving me. You ask a simple question: What's in my hand? Help me to honestly evaluate that question and to use all that You've put in my hand for Your kingdom's sake.

DAY 24

THERE IS ACCOUNTABILITY

For we must all appear before the judgment seat of Christ, so that each of us may receive what is due us for the things done while in the body, whether good or bad.

2 Corinthians 5:10

Have you heard of Enron? In 1985, in the wake of federal deregulation of natural gas pipelines, two small energy companies merged to form Enron. To complete the merger, Enron had to take on substantial debt. Enron was led by Kenneth Lay, a marketing genius with an eye for talent. One of his first key hires was a talented young consultant named Jeffrey Skilling.

Through Skilling's leadership, Enron started a series of market-making and market-leading products, including the creation of a Gas Bank. Enron created its own finance division, which led to cutting-edge deals in natural gas contracts, financing, and trading. Enron expanded into the electricity industry and, later still, into an online energy trading platform. One of its last big gambles was in internet broadband. For six years in a row, Enron was named one of Fortune's Most Innovative Companies.

Such dramatic growth doesn't come without a cost. Credit agencies demanded evidence of viability. Andrew Fastow, Enron's chief financial officer, undertook a complex series of maneuvers where he'd move assets off the books and incur significant debt. That debt was not reported on Enron's financial statements in any transparent way. Ultimately, by 2001, the glitter of a $100 billion company with twenty thousand employees began to unravel.

As regulators began to dive deep into the financial statements, they were shocked to find a sweeping lack of disclosure and hidden debt. In early 2001, Lay resigned, followed soon by Skilling and Fastow. The same dizzying rise of Enron was matched by a dizzying fall. By late 2001, Enron was bankrupt.[1] The Enron scandal, as it came to be known, proved one essential point:

There must always be an accounting.

That's a sobering truth of our lives before our God. He always requires an accounting. Every one of us will stand before Him in heaven and be held accountable for our use of His resources. There will be nothing hidden in that day. There will be no off-balance-sheet transactions. All will be laid bare before Him. And there is no skipping the accounting.

O Lord, thank You for this great truth in Your Word. We will all stand before Jesus and be held accountable for our use of the resources that You've put in our hands. Help me to be a good and wise steward, knowing that the day of accounting is coming.

DAY 25

THERE IS REWARD *and* LOSS

> Their work will be shown for what it is, because the Day will bring it to light. It will be revealed with fire, and the fire will test the quality of each person's work. If what has been built survives, the builder will receive a reward. If it is burned up, the builder will suffer loss.
>
> 1 Corinthians 3:13–15

In the previous devotional, I talked about the concept of accountability. We are all accountable before God for our use of His resources. The Legacy Life recognizes this truth. But the Legacy Life also recognizes this next great truth: there is reward and loss.

Before the Enron scandal, for fifteen years Enron was a company riding high. Its leaders—Kenneth Lay, Jeffrey Skilling, and Andrew Fastow—were paid handsomely. In one case, Fastow received a $30 million fee for putting together a deal. But the appearance was different than the reality.

Lay, Skilling, and Fastow came up with a complex accounting scheme that allowed them to hide the losses of the company. Ultimately, as regulators dug deeper into the financials, the true state of their finances came to light.

In the subsequent proceedings, Lay was convicted on ten felony counts but died of a heart attack before sentencing. Skilling ended up with a twenty-four-year sentence and served twelve years. Fastow testified against his coworkers and served five years in prison. They received their reward.[1]

The Scriptures teach a similar concept. There is a day in heaven when Christians will be held accountable for their deeds in the body. To be clear, this accountability is separate from the concept of whether we spend eternity in heaven or not. In other words, our place in heaven may be secure, but our works are still tested.

"The fire will test the quality of each person's work" (1 Cor. 3:13). There are only two results from that testing: Reward or loss. We'll either end up with a pile of ashes or pure gold. Those things that we did with a pure motive for His kingdom's sake will remain. Those things that we did for ourselves, to benefit ourselves, will wither away. I'll be the first to admit that I don't know how all of this exactly works in heaven, but I know this: In business and the kingdom, there must be an accounting, and that accounting produces reward and loss.

That thought ought to cause us to live soberly steadfast.

O Lord, thank You for reminding me that there are consequences for my actions. Reward and loss. May I live in such a way that, when the fire comes, I'll be rewarded with that which remains.

DAY 26

THE POWER *to* MAKE WEALTH

But remember the LORD your God, for it is he who gives you the ability to produce wealth, and so confirms his covenant, which he swore to your ancestors, as it is today.

Deuteronomy 8:18

At times, I've heard different people walk into some of the events we hold and describe themselves as entrepreneurs. Some have built and sold five or six companies. Sometimes I'll hear them say that they have the gift of making money. I cringe a bit when I hear that.

We've been incredibly successful at Hobby Lobby over the years. With one thousand stores across the country, one could think we've been successful. But even with Hobby Lobby, it's not like we were an overnight success. We started making frames and selling them. Then we opened a small store. Then we opened a little bigger store. Then we opened a second store. Little by little. Brick by brick.

Sometimes I like to say that we could write a book about our mistakes. One of those mistakes was when we started a furniture company. Because our Hobby Lobby stores carried some furniture items like small stands, end tables, or desks, it seemed that opening a furniture store would be a logical extension of what we did.

It made sense. We had the experience. We had the suppliers. We had the track record. We knew how to make money doing retail. So we opened our first retail furniture store, which we named Hemispheres. After opening, our sales never really took off. We tried everything—every which way of selling furniture. We used all of the retail expertise we could muster, but it never caught fire. We endured for a long time because it just seemed to make sense that we should be able to make this work.

Hemispheres eventually grew to nine stores, but it just never got over the hump. We eventually closed all nine stores. While we can point to mistakes we made, I'm also just as convinced of the truth of this Scripture: "It is he who gives you the ability to produce wealth" (Deut. 8:18).

I've seen many a person with more talent and skills than me get started and crash in flames. I've similarly seen those with lesser talent and skills watch their businesses and organizations thrive.

The Legacy Life recognizes that God is the source of our thriving. Whether it's a big business, a growing ministry, or a job we can be faithful at, He is at the center of our thriving. That recognition alone turns us to gratitude for His provision at every step of the way.

O Lord, You are the One indeed who gives the power to produce wealth in all forms. You are the source of my thriving. I'm grateful today for how You've provided for me in every way.

DAY 27

FULL *of* DAYS

> Abraham breathed his last and died at a good old age, an old man and full of years; and he was gathered to his people.
>
> Genesis 25:8

When we think of death, I doubt that we think of the word *satisfaction*. But that's the picture that I get in a few select places in Scripture.

For instance, Acts 13:36 says, "Now when David had served God's purpose in his own generation, he fell asleep." I love that idea. David served God's purpose in his time, and then it was time to go.

Or I think about Moses. From living in the palace of Pharaoh, to being cast into the wilderness, to leading the nation of Israel to deliverance, he lived quite the life. He saw firsthand the miracles of God. As his death drew near, he led the people to the verge of the promised land, and he gave his successor, Joshua, instructions for the journey ahead. Then the Scriptures record in Deuteronomy 34:7: "Moses was a hundred and twenty years old when he died, yet his eyes were not weak nor his strength gone." When I read those words, I think, *Wow!* Moses was just as vital, just as sharp at his death as he was in life. It was just time to go.

Jacob followed a similar journey. After his early squabbles with his brother, Esau, he fled empty-handed to a foreign land. There, God provided for him—a family, children, and even personal wealth. He met God in the wilderness and continued in the promise of faith made to his own father. At his death, he blessed his twelve sons. His work was done and, upon this, the Bible states, "When Jacob had finished giving instructions to his sons, he drew his feet up into the bed, breathed his last and was gathered to his people" (Gen. 49:33). Abraham's path was the same. I love the description in Genesis 25:8 that he was "full of years."

What's the point of sharing these passages? I think too often there is a fear of death—that time has run out, and there is no more life. Death is seen as a time of regret of what is not and what cannot be.

But the Scriptures flip this script on its head. Death is a time of satisfaction and contentment. We've run our course. We've completed our mission. We did what we could with what God gave us. None of it perfect, but we can breathe our last—still vital, full of days, having completed God's purpose for our life. That's the Legacy Life.

O Lord, I love Your Word and how You show us that we can run to the tape and be satisfied even at death that we've done our work—full of days and gathered to our people.

DAY 28

A GREAT ADVENTURE

> Then Asa called to the LORD his God and said, "LORD, there is no one like you to help the powerless against the mighty. Help us, LORD our God, for we rely on you, and in your name we have come against this vast army. LORD, you are our God; do not let mere mortals prevail against you."
>
> 2 Chronicles 14:11

My son Mart will sometimes start a talk by asking a question: "How many of you want to live a great adventure?" The room will fill with upraised hands. Then he'll follow that question with: "How many of you want to live a dangerous and uncertain undertaking?" Not many hands will shoot up. But he'll cap it by saying that an adventure is a dangerous and uncertain undertaking.

When we sued the federal government in 2012, we knew that we might lose the company if we lost the lawsuit. During that lawsuit and even following it, we received stacks of mail sometimes two to three feet high. Most of it was hate mail. There were countless newspaper articles. Again, most of it was negative. We felt outnumbered, even as we remained assured of our position. For me, an Oklahoma barely-high-school graduate, it was a surreal feeling to walk out onto the steps of the United States Supreme Court with our case as the one in focus.

King Asa had that same kind of feeling. The Cushites came to attack in full force with a million men and three hundred chariots. Asa was outnumbered by almost two to one. His little army must have trembled at the sight of the vast horde in front of them. Is it any wonder that Asa cries out, "LORD, there is no one like you to help the powerless against the mighty" (2 Chron. 14:11)?

In the verses that follow Asa's powerful prayer, God, in a matter-of-fact fashion, dispenses with the Cushite army. They flee. So great is the victory that the Israelites descend on nearby towns and gain additional victories and carry off great plunder.

The Legacy Life is a great adventure. When we follow Christ, we don't always know where the road will turn. Sometimes it truly does seem that it is the mighty against the few. Sometimes God's path is through the sea, His way through the mighty waters, even if His footprints are unseen (Ps. 77:19).

But in the bigger picture, God always gives the victory. It may not be in the manner or the time that we imagine, but He always brings it. Think about that. Someday when we see King Asa in heaven, I'm sure he'll tell us the story of the great victory. To live the adventure, however, we've got to go through uncertainty. We've got to experience the unknown, even the dangerous.

O Lord, I call upon Your name. You are the God of the weak and the powerless against the mighty. You deliver victory through Your own hand. May we live this great adventure with You.

DAY 29

THE ORDINARY DAYS

> He said to the senior servant in his household, the one in charge of all that he had . . .
>
> Genesis 24:2

It's easy to get lost in all this legacy talk. We can certainly become enamored with the heroes of the faith—Abraham, Isaac, Jacob, Moses, Joshua, David . . . the list could go on and on.

It's easy to look at someone like David and think, *Well, he fought Goliath. He was a warrior king, and he wrote the Psalms. Or what about Moses—he wrote the first five books of the Bible, and he was up on the mountain meeting with God. Joshua fought the battle of Jericho!* We can have all kinds of hero worship.

Perhaps we might ask: What about me? I'm not one of those famous guys.

I was like that. I was the poor pastor's kid. We had to work to get food on the table and the house furnished.

I remember there was this one kid in the band. He was the cool trumpet player. His pants had the neatest crease. His hair was slicked back, and he had an air of confidence about him. He was at the top of the food chain. I was a tuba player. I mean, who asks a tuba player to do a solo? One day, I'd had enough of that trumpet player, and we got into a little tussle. Let's just say I didn't do too well.

What's the point? The Legacy Life isn't about fame, or the great exploits and adventures you undertake. It's not about being at the top of the food chain, or whether you play a trumpet or a tuba, or even whether you have creases in your pants. The Legacy Life is about one thousand ordinary days of just being faithful with your assignment.

I love the story in Genesis where Abraham's son Isaac needed a wife. So, Abraham called his servant and sent him on a mission. He made his servant swear that he would not let his son marry a Canaanite woman, as she would be from a people who did not worship God. The servant went to Abraham's original homeland and, in an act of providence, was met by a woman who helped him water his camels. That woman proved to be one of Abraham's own people and became Isaac's wife.

The Ordinary Days

What I love most about this story is that we never know the servant's name. He's not famous like his master, Abraham, or like the son, Isaac, or like any of those who would follow after. He is the unnamed servant. But because he was faithful, Isaac had a son, Jacob, who was renamed Israel, and the story continues today.

I think about that for our own lives. Most of us will never make newspaper headlines, pitch in a major league baseball game, kick a soccer ball in a World Cup match, or stand on a stage preaching a message. Life is about a bunch of ordinary days. Sometimes it's working the line at the factory. Or putting shipping tape on a box or crunching numbers on a computer.

That's the Legacy Life. Sometimes we get simple missions, sometimes inconvenient ones, and it might be easy to complain about the apparent mundanity. But God uses those missions to shape entire worlds around us.

O Lord, thank You for the unnamed servant who was faithful with his mission. He lived the Legacy Life. Help me to be faithful with all my ordinary assignments.

DAY 30

TELL *the* GENERATIONS

> He decreed statutes for Jacob and established the law in Israel, which he commanded our ancestors to teach their children, so the next generation would know them, even the children yet to be born, and they in turn would tell their children. Then they would put their trust in God and would not forget his deeds but would keep his commands.
>
> Psalm 78:5–7

Have you ever thought about being a five-generation family? A seven-generation family? A fifteen-generation family? For most of us, that's inconceivable. It's enough to think about getting the kids off to school, or out of high school and on to successful careers.

But there are societies of businesses in Europe where you don't gain admission until you've been in business for two hundred years or more. I've had occasion to travel to Europe, and it's always amazing to see buildings and streets that have been in existence longer than America as a nation has been around.

That's why I love Psalm 78. It gives us the generational picture of God's design. Note the steps:

> Our ancestors should teach their children,
> Who should teach the next generation,
> Who should teach the children yet unborn,
> Who should tell their children.

If you are keeping track, that's five generations. Our ancestors. Their children. The next generation. The children not yet born. And the next generation.

What are they supposed to do? Teach God's statutes or, to put it differently, teach the way of life in God. For five generations. What is the big why? Why are they supposed to teach God's way? The answer is found in verse seven: so that they would put their trust in God.

Notably, Psalm 78 isn't written by David. It's written by Asaph. He was the chief musician in David's court. He continued as chief musician for Solomon. And some suggest he lived to see the fall of Solomon's son Rehoboam. Asaph writes with a generational perspective. He saw the generations rise and fall. He'd seen Israel rise and fall in their own faithfulness. If we fast-forward, we see Asaph's sons at the rebuilding of the wall in the book of Nehemiah—perhaps four hundred years of faithfulness.

Can you imagine the impact of five generations of faithfulness? Can you imagine your children telling your grandchildren who tell your great-grandchildren who tell your great-great-grandchildren of the goodness of God?

O Lord, give me the vision for generations of people who follow after me. Give me the vision for one generation after the next who is still sharing Your goodness from one generation to the next.

PART 2
The LEGACY PRACTICES

DAY 31

THE LEGACY CLOCK

Teach us to number our days, that we may gain a heart of wisdom.

Psalm 90:12

Do you know what a legacy clock is? It's a clock that numbers our days.

When we begin this journey of life, we have no concept of time. Our early school years are marked by the cycles of school starting and school ending. But by the time our teens and twenties come, we are off to the races. Our thirties are often the time of establishing and our forties are a time of honing, while our fifties are a time of reflecting. Maybe by our sixties we are starting to look back.

Meanwhile, the legacy clock has been running all along. No one knows how long they have on this earth. Even at the time of this writing, a good friend called to tell me about his cancer diagnosis. He's got maybe three to four months. And our children? Well, we've got eighteen summers before they are off on their own. Eighteen summers and that's it. After that we have to start to chase them a bit. When they have their own children, it gets more and more crazy. Life gets juggled around work schedules, sports schedules, school schedules, and sick kid schedules.

Put differently, from birth to age eighteen, we have 6,570 days. We don't get any back once they are gone. I know of one family whose goal is to have each kid have one thousand extraordinary days before age eighteen. Those extraordinary days can be however you define them—a soccer match, a piano recital, a unique trip, a mission trip. The key is to be intentional. If you've got young children, you've got to start now, and you've got to plan for those extraordinary days.

If you've got adult children, then the equation changes dramatically. After age eighteen, your children spend less and less time with you. After they get married, it's far less still, and if they move out of state, perhaps it's one week out of the year. So, if you've got twenty-five years' worth of seven days, then you've got a chance for 175 extraordinary days maximum. That's sobering.

What about your own life? How many years do you have? Ten? Twenty? Thirty? Forty? How many extraordinary days do you have? How many do you want to have? The legacy clock is ticking.

The first step of your plan is to realize the clock is ticking. You don't have forever. Particularly in our youth, we think the runway is forever. We give little thought to the fact that our days are numbered. The second step is to make a plan. It will take work, thought, and time to lay out your legacy plan—all while the clock is ticking. That's why I think the psalmist encourages us and challenges us: "Teach us to number our days" (Ps. 90:12).

O Lord, I confess that I'm prone to think that my days are unlimited. I confess that I don't like to think about my death and departure from this planet. Help me, I pray, to take the time to plan and prepare for extraordinary days as long as I have life and breath.

DAY 32

RESET YOUR THINKING

Know therefore that the LORD your God is God; he is the faithful God, keeping his covenant of love to a thousand generations of those who love him and keep his commandments.

Deuteronomy 7:9

Living a Legacy Life takes more than inspiration. Over my now more than eighty years, I've seen the world change dramatically. We've moved from a place of family and community to a singular focus on the individual.

When I was growing up in the 1940s, it seemed like everyone was poor. Our neighbors scratched away at their little farms and they brought us their poundings—pounds of potatoes, turnips, tomatoes, or green beans. They shared what they had as part of their tithe. While the rations we received might have seemed meager pickings, they were sacrificial for the families that brought them. We were part of a bigger church family.

In our family, we truly had to share our house. It meant that my sisters got the bedroom, the boys slept in the kitchen, and my parents slept in the living room. I don't feel deprived by that experience. I feel blessed. Sharing life together like that meant that the ministry of the church moved forward.

If we needed something as a family, we went to work for it together. That's where I learned to pick cotton. We'd go out during the season as a family and pick cotton. As the fifth child, I was always trying to keep up with my other brothers and sisters, which was no easy task. At the end of the season, we'd pool our earnings, and we could go buy that piece of furniture we needed—a new couch or a new kitchen table. Those purchases meant something to us as a group because we did it together.

Our Western world today has preached mightily about the rights of the individual. We almost think it sacrilege today if our kids can't have their own bedrooms or playrooms. We so want to tailor our parenting to the gifts of each child that we sometimes wear ourselves out with piano lessons, gymnastics classes, math competitions, debate tournaments, soccer try-outs, and so on.

The family is not a nest we launch our children from to a life of pursuing their own dreams. The notion of letting our kids spread their wings and fly should be balanced by the proverb that we want to help our children find roots as well as wings. We are all rooted in a big story of family, of generations—most of whom we never knew—to bring us to this day.

Our aim should be to raise our children to realize they are part of a big family, a big, ongoing story. It's not perfect. But it is our story, and it's a privilege to be part of that story. And we need each other!

O Lord, we love Your Word. We love the idea that we should think about a thousand generations and not just our lives, ourselves, and our kids. There's a bigger story.

DAY 33

BE CONTENT

> I have learned the secret of being content.
>
> Philippians 4:12

I've not had a raise in twenty years. And it's not because I haven't earned a raise.

If I were working for another company, my salary would probably be about twenty times what it is. Or more. Sometimes when we do a CEO event with Bill, he'll stop and ask me, "Why? Why give 50 percent of your profit away? You could make the case for buying a second house, a third house, an island somewhere, or even simply investing more in Hobby Lobby."

For the longest time, I struggled with how best to answer that question. Over the years, I've answered that question in lots of different ways. But finally, the simplest answer occurred to me: I'm content.

There's nothing that this world has that I need.

Do I need another car? (I've got enough.) Do I need a boat? (I don't think so!) Another house? (It's just one more thing to maintain.) Do I need a country club membership? (I don't play golf!)

No matter how you dress up the things of this world, there's simply no appeal for me. Now, don't get me wrong, it's not that I don't enjoy going out to a good restaurant and having a nice meal, but the things of this world are all part of the vapor of life. They disappear.

The apostle Paul says, "I've learned the secret of being content" (Phil. 4:12). Contentment is a learned art. We train ourselves to turn away from the glitter of the world. I remember the words of the old hymn "Turn Your Eyes Upon Jesus":

> Turn your eyes upon Jesus,
> Look full in his wonderful face,
> And the things of this earth will grow strangely
> dim,
> In the light of his glory and grace.

What about you? What catches your attention? Have you been caught in the allure of the world? What's your appetite for? Is it more of the things of this world? Or is it more of God? Is it more of the things of eternity?

Be Content

As we learn the secrets of contentment, we build the foundations of the Legacy Life and a life pointing to that day in heaven.

O Lord, teach me, I cry out to You, that I might learn the secrets of the life of contentment—a life focused on You, and not on the things of this world. Let the things of this earth indeed grow strangely dim in the light of Your glory and grace.

DAY 34

A REGULAR FAMILY MEETING

> Six days you shall labor and do all your work, but the seventh day is a sabbath to the LORD your God. On it you shall not do any work.
>
> Exodus 20:9–10

Rhythms are predictable patterns of behavior. One of the biggest and most important rhythms is the Sabbath.

What's the Sabbath? It's a time when we stop working. Let those two words sink in: *stop working*. We stop working, we take time to fellowship with friends and family, and we remember what God has done.

In our modern world, we tend not to have an appreciation for the idea of a Sabbath. I've been privileged to visit Israel on two or three occasions. I was always amazed that, still to this day, once Friday evening came around, Israel went into shutdown mode. But, wow, once Sabbath ended, there was music, food, laughing, people gathering on street corners. It was a party!

That's the power of setting aside time each week. A time for yourself to stop working. To focus on family and recalibrate. It's the family meeting. As families focus on their vision, mission, and values, they often take time to set a regular family meeting. The family meeting is not just a fun time. It's a time to discuss the business of family (not the family business).

The business of family regards things like personal updates—what's going on in each family member's world. Too often we assume that we know what's occurred in each person's life. It's a great time to check in on any interpersonal issues—is anyone hurting or experiencing strained relationships? Other agenda items might include family goals, projects the family is working on, ministry service opportunities, family finances, and coordinating schedules.

A regular family meeting is also a great place to review our vision and values statements, as well as giving opportunities. Sometimes people will ask me how old a child should be before they are included in family giving. I say the sooner the better. To develop the giving habit, children need to see it demonstrated and be given the right to participate. It's one of the most powerful habits you can build in your children.

Family meetings can match the pace of your own family. For younger families it might be weekly. For older children it might be once or twice a month. For adult children, it might be quarterly or twice a year. No doubt the family that meets together develops one of the most powerful rhythms we can have.

O Lord, thank You for reminding me of the Sabbath and the power of a regular rhythm with my family. Help me institute this concept of a family meeting in my own family.

DAY 35

GROUNDED *in* FAITH

> That person is like a tree planted by streams of water, which yields its fruit in season and whose leaf does not wither—whatever they do prospers.
>
> Psalm 1:3

Sometimes when we look around in our world, it's easy to compare ourselves to others. We can look across the fence and see our neighbors and sure wish that we could have a car like theirs. Or maybe it seems like they've got the perfect marriage and the perfect kids.

We live in a celebrity culture, where we can look at a stage, the big screen, or countless social media posts and think, *Wow, I wish I could live a life like that: Perfect hair, cool clothes, great food, and plenty of money.*

But I've seen behind those headlines. I remember not too long ago being with one of those couples. They'd stood on stages, moving and inspiring others in their faith. They had multiple houses and kids who seemed put together, and the dollars were flowing in. Underneath, however, was a very different story. Their marriage was disconnected. Their kids felt it. One had already walked away from the faith. The other was on the verge of it. There was a mountain of debt, and it seemed the divorce papers weren't too far away.

I know this: Life is hard. The storms will come. The Scriptures tell us so. Isaiah 43:2 says, "When you pass through the waters . . . when you pass through the rivers . . . When you walk through the fire." It's not *if* you face hard times; it's a matter of *when*.

Rich or poor, famous or unknown, celebrity or ordinary person, married or single—you could go on and on. Life happens to all. Is it any wonder that in Ecclesiastes 9:11 the writer says, "The race is not to the swift or the battle to the strong, nor does food come to the wise or wealth to the brilliant or favor to the learned; but time and chance happen to them all"?

When you look over the fence at your neighbor, just remember they are having the same struggles that you are! What is the key? What is the difference? If you want to lead and live the Legacy Life, the life that matters, the life that lasts, you'll remember that *it is only the life grounded in faith that thrives in the long run.*

Psalm 1:3 teaches us that a faith-filled person is like a tree planted by streams of water. That's a promise for the life of faith. When you are by the stream, you'll always have water. You can endure the hard times that will inevitably come. Your leaves will not wither. Instead, you'll prosper and you'll bear fruit.

It's a life decision. Ground your life in faith. For all time.

O Lord, we love Your Word and the instruction it gives. We ground our lives in faith. We are planted in faith by Your streams of water.

DAY 36

ELIMINATE *the* "AND"

Forgetting what is behind and straining toward what is ahead, I press on toward the goal to win the prize for which God has called me heavenward in Christ Jesus.

Philippians 3:13–14

"I'd like to figure out how I can make my first million. Then I can retire and do ministry stuff."

That was how a young man started a conversation with me. He was bright, articulate, and focused. I couldn't help but admire his drive. But I was bothered.

I remember years ago reading A. W. Tozer's *The Pursuit of God*. There is a line that has stuck with me many years later: "The evil habit of seeking *God-and* effectively prevents us from finding God in full revelation. In the 'and' lies our great woe."[1]

What did Tozer mean by seeking "God-and"? It means we want God *and* our first million, *and* a healthy

401(k), *and* a comfortable house, *and* neat vacations, *and* the cutest kids. Perhaps you've got another *and* on your list. I think we need to seriously evaluate our *and*'s. Tozer's warning is noteworthy: In the "and" lies our great woe.

I'm afraid that this "God-and" is much of what we see in this world today. We only want God in parts of our life—those parts where things are comfortable and good. We want God to inspire us, to give us nuggets from His Word, and only when times are tough do we seek Him out in prayer.

Even when pressed about how the love of money is the root of all evil, many of us would jokingly laugh, "Yes, but I'm sure it wouldn't be for me." That's why lottery ticket sales never stagnate.

But we do not let God into those areas where we might find conviction of sin, where He might challenge us on our behaviors. Stuck habits. Quiet addictions. Private viewings. The extra glass of wine. I might ask: Where are the warriors? Where are the dreamers? Where are those who might leave their comfort and go to the farthest ends of the earth for the sake of the gospel? Where are those who are willing to give up their ownership for a greater call?

Let us throw open the doors of our life and let God invade every room. Let us call out to Him that He is enough. He alone is all that our hearts desire. More than gold, more than the things of this world, more than *and*.

O Lord, we invite You in to deeply examine the wants and the and*'s of our life. And we cry out to You to eliminate them in favor of a life of You alone.*

DAY 37

FIRST THINGS FIRST

In the morning, LORD, you hear my voice; in the morning I lay my requests before you and wait expectantly.

Psalm 5:3

Have you heard the phrase that whatever you sow in kind, you'll reap in multiples? If you have ever planted a tomato plant, you know what I mean. One little tomato plant can yield what seems like hundreds of tomatoes. Pretty soon that little plant might mean that you need to find new friends who will take your leftover tomatoes.

In my own life, I've tried to plant tomato plants. What do I mean? Sometimes what you plant in your own life, you reap in multiples in generations to come. In beginning our married life, Barbara and I knew that we wanted to base our life on the power of God's Word. It is the foundation of the Legacy Life. We sank our roots deep into the local church, and we exposed our family to other families on the same journey.

In our own marriage, we seek to begin every day in God's Word. We go through a devotional together and ground ourselves there. God's Word gives us wisdom for the day. True to God's promise, His Word yields in multiples.

That simple act of being in God's Word every single day as a first priority has meant so much in my life. Today, there are three guiding principles for my life that come straight from Scripture. The first is that God says He will never leave us or forsake us (Deut. 31:8). The second is that we have not because we ask not (James 4:2). The third is that we should pray without ceasing (1 Thess. 5:17).

Those principles have impacted how I run Hobby Lobby, and I believe without a doubt they have impacted our growth. That growth has allowed us to work with thousands of vendors around the world and to employ thousands of employees. That growth has allowed us to be generous and to support ministries around the world. We believe there have been millions of people who have responded to the gospel.

That's the power of beginning every day with God's Word. It yields in multiples.

My encouragement to you is to plant a tomato plant. Plant God's Word in your family. Make God's Word the very first priority in your own life. Read it daily. Expose your children to a Bible-teaching church.

As the roots of God's Word grow deep in the lives of your children, you'll be planting tomato plants. The yield in one generation will be incredible, but far more in the generations to come.

O Lord, help me to plant tomato plants—to make Your Word first in my life every single day and to trust You for the harvest.

DAY 38

GROUNDED *in* GOD'S WORD

When your words came, I ate them; they were my joy and my heart's delight, for I bear your name, LORD God Almighty.

Jeremiah 15:16

Barbara and I have been married for over sixty years. We've become creatures of habit. One of our favorite things is to go out and have dinner. But when you've been married for as long as we have, sometimes you get stuck on where you want to go out and eat. So I keep tucked in my back pocket a little book I call My Pad. One part of My Pad is a list of restaurants. If we ever get stuck on where we might go out to eat, we just pull out My Pad and review our options. It works for us.

In the same way that we go out to eat, there's a deeper nutrition that each one of us needs every single day. That's God's Word. As I mentioned in the previous devotion, I start every day with devotional time. Many times, it's with Barbara as we sit and have a cup of coffee and a bagel. It helps me set my mind for the day. I seek to live in the truth and grace of God's Word every single day.

My son Mart tells the story of traveling to Guatemala to be part of a Bible dedication ceremony. It had taken fifty long years to complete the translation. Sometimes there were delays. For instance, guerrillas burned down the house of the missionaries working on the translation. They didn't want the natives to learn to read. As part of the ceremony, Mart saw something he'd never seen before: a man named Gaspar came forward to receive the very first Bible in his own language, and as he came, he wept.

That moment changed Mart. He realized that he'd never wept over the privilege of having his own Bible. From that day forward, he committed to reading God's Word as his first priority every day.

For my son Steve, he's always been fascinated by the study of God's Word. Despite a busy travel schedule, he still loves to study and prepare for teaching Sunday school. He's written a book called *This Beautiful Book* where he shows how the Bible is one story. Although it has thirty-six different authors with sixty-six books and was written over fifteen hundred years, the Bible has one central theme: How God seeks to provide a means of redemption and restoration through His Son Jesus Christ.

The prophet Jeremiah says that as he "eats" God's Word, it produces joy and delight. I think the term is appropriate. Eating is something we want to do! Three times a day or more. As I write, I can think of no greater encouragement to those reading these words. Do you want to live a Legacy Life? Do you want to live a life of meaning? Of significance?

Then commit to taking in God's Word every single day. Read it. Study it. Listen to it. Memorize it. You will build a life of wisdom, joy, and delight.

O Lord, thank You for giving us Your Word. May I commit to going deeper in Your Word this day and all the days to come.

DAY 39

READ *for* CONTEXT— NOT JUST NUGGETS

> He said to them, "This is what I told you while I was still with you: Everything must be fulfilled that is written about me in the Law of Moses, the Prophets and the Psalms."
>
> Luke 24:44

My son Steve makes it a practice to read through the Bible—cover to cover—every single year. Why does he read that way? He sees it as one story.

Some read the Bible for nuggets. They have issues in their life, so they want to find comfort. Or maybe they have a major trial in their life, so they read to find verses about persevering. Or still others employ a more random approach—letting the Bible fall open to some new passage or verse of the day.

I remember hearing the story of a man who let his Bible fall open to Matthew 27:5: "Then he went away and hanged himself." Unsatisfied with this verse, he tried again, and his finger landed upon Luke 10:37: "Go and do likewise." Now unnerved, he gave it one more try and landed upon John 13:27: "What you are about to do, do it quickly." He gave up on the fully random approach after that experience.

I think that's why we tend to get bogged down in the Old Testament. If we see the Law as a series of irrelevant laws, for instance, we'll never make it through them. While the stories of the judges make for some interesting reading, we might wonder about how they apply to us today. Or the endless genealogies might provide for a place for easy speed-reading.

But when we read the Bible for context, when we read it as one story, we start to see the larger themes. The genealogies tell us that God valued a family line. They tell us we are part of something—we came from a larger story. We are not mere individuals alone on an island. The lives of the kings tell us that, no matter how great the king, we cannot save ourselves. And what about the endless laws? They tell us that God wants us to live by a code—a way of life that is different from the rest of the world.

I've heard others say it this way: we should read the gospel on every page of the Bible. That's how Jesus saw the Bible. That's what He essentially said in Luke 24:44—look for the gospel in the Law of Moses, the Prophets, and the Psalms. When we read for context, we begin to make the connections from Genesis to Revelation. The drumbeat of redemption and restoration runs throughout.

When we see the context of Scripture, we realize in the same way that our lives are connected to one another. We need one another. We need our families. We need our church community. We impact one another. We realize that we are putting a legacy in motion.

O Lord, help me to read Your Word as one big story, connected from beginning to end. Help us read for context and not just nuggets.

DAY 40

GROUNDED *in* CONTINUAL PRAYER

Pray continually.

1 Thessalonians 5:17

The Legacy Life starts with God's Word. Take it in. Gain nourishment and wisdom from it. Go deep with it.

Then pray. Pray at appointed times. Perhaps you're a regular morning or evening devotion kind of person, and prayer is part of your routine. By all means, keep doing that. We see Daniel in the Old Testament set three times for prayer each day (Dan. 6:10). For some that might be a morning, noon, and night prayer—a conscious effort of setting aside time for prayer.

Or you could pray in the watches of the night. King David said it this way in Psalm 63:6: "On my bed I remember you; I think of you through the watches of the

Grounded in Continual Prayer

night." That psalm was written when David was in the wilderness of Judah. They had to set watches during the night to protect them from the enemy. I can almost imagine one of the watchmen calling out, "All is well." And with it a prayer was lifted up.

My wife Barbara prays that God will wake her during the night so she can pray. (I confess that I don't pray for that particular gift because I like to get my sleep!) But she'll wake up, sit in her prayer closet, put on her prayer shawl, and journal. She's got dozens of journals of times when God has spoken to her.

Certainly, we should pray in times of darkness when the enemy comes upon us. Asa prayed in the midst of battle: "LORD, there is no one like you to help the powerless against the mighty" (2 Chron. 14:11). We should pray like Jesus, away from the crowds and in the silence: "After leaving them, he went up on a mountainside to pray" (Mark 6:46).

Are you getting the point? The idea that Paul summed up in 1 Thessalonians 5:17 is to "pray continually." Another translation is "pray without ceasing" (ESV). Paul repeated the idea in Romans 12:12 as being "faithful in prayer." Or in Colossians 4:2, he says, "Devote yourselves to prayer." In Ephesians 6:18, he says, "Pray in the Spirit on all occasions."

That's what I imagine day by day. That Jesus is with me, moment by moment, walking and talking with me. He wants to invade my life. He wants to speak into every single area of my life.

That's why the apostle Paul could say, "I have been crucified with Christ and I no longer live, but Christ lives in me" (Gal. 2:20). It is a lifelong aspiration that I pray daily and continually in the Spirit.

O Lord, my heart's prayer is that You might teach me to pray this way—praying continually, praying without ceasing.

DAY 41

CULTIVATE *and* OBEY HOLY SPIRIT NUDGES

> But the Advocate, the Holy Spirit, whom the Father will send in my name, will teach you all things and will remind you of everything I have said to you.
>
> John 14:26

All it takes is a few seconds of insane courage to change your life. That's what my wife Barbara says when she begins a presentation.

I call those few seconds of courage Holy Spirit nudges. Those nudges are the moments when God speaks to you. It doesn't mean that it's an audible voice, but it's like He's right there at your elbow. He's the whisper in your spirit and the prick of your conscience.

Those nudges might look like the Holy Spirit telling you to reach out to that friend, make that call, send that card or letter, get down on your knees and pray, or maybe send that financial gift you've been asked to

The Legacy Practices

make. That's the role of the Holy Spirit: He's our advocate, our helper. He provides us direction.

The Scriptures show us so many of those nudges. It's Jonathan and his armor bearer being called into battle (1 Sam. 14:12). It's King David holding back on delivering punishment to Shimei (2 Sam. 16:11). It's Esther taking the risk to go before the king and to plead for her people (Esther 4:16). It's Abraham being willing to leave his family and homeland to go to a new country (Rom. 4:2–21).

We cultivate those nudges by listening, paying attention, and being in an attitude of prayer. And we encourage those nudges by obeying them. They may not always make sense. In my own life, God has asked me to start a business with a $600 loan, to give $30,000 when I didn't have it, and to try to outgive God. Sometimes those nudges are points of correction—like my pride or my need for gratitude. I can trust, however, that as I obey those nudges, there'll be more of them.

We can also quench those nudges. Sometimes God will bring us things and we'll think, "No way. He's not really asking me to do that!" Or sometimes we'll say, "Aw, I'm tired. Can I wait until I have more energy?" It makes me wonder what would have happened if Moses had never turned aside to look at the burning bush. Or what would have happened if Daniel had just fallen in line and chosen not to pray.

How are you doing with the nudges in your life? Can you take a look back and see the times when you heard or felt a nudge from the Holy Spirit? Can you think of a time when you obeyed that nudge? Or a time when you did not? There's so much freedom when we respond to the nudge. I think God is always pleased by those who are willing to take a risk for Him. I don't think we'll get to heaven and say, "Wow, I wish I would have risked less and listened to fewer nudges from the Holy Spirit."

O Lord, help me through Your Word and through prayer to listen and obey the nudges from Your Holy Spirit.

DAY 42

TAKE *the* RISK

> I have been constantly on the move. I have been in danger from rivers, in danger from bandits, in danger from my fellow Jews, in danger from Gentiles; in danger in the city, in danger in the country, in danger at sea; and in danger from false believers.
>
> 2 Corinthians 11:26

Wouldn't it have been great to be the apostle Paul? Think of it. He lived in the pioneering days of the church. It must have been exciting to be on the forefront. Or think again!

In this short little passage from 2 Corinthians, we know that Paul took a risk for the gospel. It meant that at times he fled for his life. He faced danger from the weather, danger from lawless men, danger from his fellow countrymen. In fact, danger was pretty much everywhere he went.

Was the risk worth it? It is if you believe in the Legacy Life and fruit of the harvest that Paul will see in heaven.

Everyone says they want to live a great adventure. When they think of adventure, they think perhaps of the wind blowing in their hair as they ride along a frothy surf in some sailboat. Sounds like fun, doesn't it? But adventure involves risk.

Adventure means not knowing the outcome. Sometimes it is that thin, fine line between loss and safety. It's a willingness to undergo uncertainty. Some might look at the breadth of Hobby Lobby's success and think it is easy to take risks. That's misleading because there were a thousand times when we didn't know what the outcome would be.

A few years ago, at the start of the global pandemic, we saw a significant increase in sales. As money flooded into the hands of the public and the pent-up demand was released, sales peaked. I took a risk and dramatically increased our buying of Christmas merchandise. I thought these big sales would continue. They didn't. Was the risk worth it? In the short term, it wasn't a lot of fun, but the situation forced us to look at ourselves and make adjustments that would benefit us in the long run.

That's the way it is with risk. We look backward to learn from it, but it helps us live forward.

I know this: there are those reading these pages who've had similar opportunities for adventure. Fear holds them back. Taking the risk may mean stepping up, stepping out, speaking up, speaking out. You'll know in that moment, and you'll sense God's pleasure as you take that next step. His Spirit will guide you.

O Lord, I'm reminded that You are a God who takes pleasure in those who are willing to take risks for You. Would You renew in me and my heart, by Your Holy Spirit, the willingness to take on the new adventures that You have for me? I believe they are big and bold!

DAY 43

WRITE DOWN YOUR VISION

> Write down the revelation and make it plain on tablets
> so that a herald may run with it.
>
> Habakkuk 2:2

It's a famous verse. Write the vision down. But few of us do it. We tend to go through life like Forrest Gump—like feathers floating in the wind.

What is vision? Vision is creating a picture of an ideal future state. People, families, and organizations struggle for lack of vision. They lack a picture of where they are going.

When I look at Jesus, I see Him constantly driving toward one central vision for His disciples: "Therefore go and make disciples of all nations, baptizing them in the name of the Father and of the Son and of the Holy Spirit" (Matt. 28:19–20).

Why was this vision so essential? The disciples loved being around Jesus, but they often got confused. They loved the limelight, but they ultimately thought He'd free them from the oppression of Rome. But He taught them about a very different kind of kingdom, one where love and mercy prevailed—not power and might.

Despite their confusion, He kept pointing them to this different kind of kingdom. Ultimately, He gave them the vision of making disciples of all nations. They understood the concept of disciple-making. It simply meant making more groups like the one they'd been part of for three years—groups of Christ followers. They were to replicate those groups in all nations.

When Jesus departed, they knew exactly what to do: Make disciples. They started in Jerusalem—right where they lived—and they began to expand outward from there. They understood the vision.

I'm a pretty simple guy. My vision for my life at the beginning was to have a great marriage, a great family, and a great career. For our family, we've got a very specific vision statement that defines our desire to impact the world for Christ. My coauthor, Bill, has his vision statement down to four words: Disciples everywhere for generations. Here's the point: You may adopt the vision statement that Jesus had for His disciples. Or you may elect to craft a vision statement specifically for your life and your family.

If you create a clear picture of the vision for your life and family, it gets everyone engaged. It's something to be a part of and to get excited about. Think in big terms just like Jesus—all nations. Not some but all! Write your vision statement down and share it. Shorter is better. Talk about it often. It will guide your practice and life.

Those who paint a picture for the future and write it down increase their chances for success.

O Lord, help me paint the picture for myself, my children, and future generations of this call to follow You from generation to generation.

DAY 44

LIFE *on* MISSION

> I have brought you glory on earth by finishing the work you gave me to do.
>
> John 17:4

A few years back, Rick Warren wrote a book that sold more than fifty million copies and was translated into over one hundred languages. This book, *The Purpose Driven Life*, is based on one of the most basic questions in all of life: What on earth are you here for? That question of purpose—of mission—is essential to all of life.

What drives you on a day-to-day basis?

In business, we call it a mission statement. Now, this is a little different than the vision statement we discussed in the previous devotional. While a vision statement is a big, bold, exciting, forward-looking dream, a mission statement is a short little statement of purpose that tells us what we should do every single day. A few short examples are from Kickstarter, "To help bring creative projects to life"; Google, "To organize the world's information and make it universally accessible and useful"; and Sony, "To be a company that inspires and fulfills your curiosity."[1]

Oddly, while we have mission statements for our businesses, our nonprofits, and our churches, we often don't have one for our lives or our families. We are far more intentional about our businesses than our lives.

Yet throughout Scripture, we see God giving clear mission statements to people. For John the Baptist, it was "to prepare the way" (Luke 1:76). For the apostle Paul, it was to proclaim God's name before Israel, the Gentiles, and kings (Acts 9:15). For Jeremiah, it was to be a prophet to the nations (Jer. 1:5). For Moses, it was to deliver God's people (Exod. 3:10). For Isaiah, it was to "go and tell" (Isa. 6:9). For Jesus, it was to train the Twelve—that's why He could say that He finished the work that God gave Him to do in John 17:4.

In a similar way, we, too, should have our own mission statement. And while John the Baptist, Paul, Jeremiah, Moses, and Isaiah had very specific callings, Jesus provided us clear examples of mission statements in the instructions He gave to the disciples. For instance, at the beginning of their journey, He told them, "Come, follow me . . . and I will send you out to fish for people" (Matt. 4:19). Later, He gave them something more specific: "Take up [your] cross daily" (Luke 9:23). Or in Matthew 6:33, He said, "Seek first [God's] kingdom and his righteousness."

Our family has our own mission statement. It's all focused on walking with God and living out our faith. It can be passed on from generation to generation. Let me encourage you to take the cue. The most successful people and the most successful families wake up and answer the question: What am I here on earth for?

It's usually a short little statement like you've seen above. Nothing magical but practical. To know Christ and make Him known, for instance. It need not be original. It just needs to be written down.

O Lord, help me to be practical in my faith and to be clear about my purpose with a simple, clear mission statement written down.

DAY 45

RITUALS *and* RHYTHMS

> They devoted themselves to the apostles' teaching and to fellowship, to the breaking of bread and to prayer. . . . All the believers were together and had everything in common. . . . Every day they continued to meet together in the temple courts. They broke bread in their homes and ate together with glad and sincere hearts, praising God and enjoying the favor of all the people.
>
> Acts 2:42, 44, 46–47

I'll admit that while I never got to play sports as a kid, I like watching college and professional football. Some of what intrigues me about the game of football is that generally everyone has the same basic plays—runs up the middle, end-arounds, short passes, long passes, and so on. Even though everyone has the same basic playbook, there are some teams who are consistently better.

What's the difference? It's the coach. A coach who implements a system with regular rituals and rhythms will always win, no matter the team, the division, or the players. They'll find a way to win.

I find it the same in business, in family, and in our day-to-day life. Those people who have a system always win. In our business, for instance, we meet on the first Wednesday of every month. We have a broad leadership meeting where we update everyone on the status of the company and the ministry. Then we have an officer's meeting. We follow that with a family meeting where we talk about giving. Every single month.

As a family, we have quarterly birthday celebrations. And we have an annual family celebration. It's a pretty simple plan. When our kids were younger, we could count on a spring trip and a summer trip. These were the rituals and rhythms of our family.

If you want to live the Legacy Life, both as an individual and as a family, you'll need the same kinds of rituals and rhythms. Some of them will occur daily—time in God's Word, time in prayer, time with your spouse and children. Some of them will be weekly—time in church, time for fun, time for exercise. Some will be monthly—time to work as a family, time to play together, time to serve.

Rituals and Rhythms

These patterns need not be numerous. They just need to be consistent. These predictable patterns help us build strength in our habits and behavior, so that when times of testing come, we can turn to that strength. For our children, these rhythms give them something they can count on. In a world so full of noise and activity, it helps build a safety net.

Is it any wonder that the early church grew? They had rhythms and rituals—breaking bread, fellowshiping, teaching God's Word, gathering together. These rhythms make us strong.

O Lord, help me to establish predictable patterns of behavior for my life and family—daily, weekly, monthly, seasonally, and annually—to build strength and safety.

DAY 46

THE POWER *of* CELEBRATION

David and all Israel were celebrating with all their might before the LORD, with castanets, harps, lyres, timbrels, sistrums and cymbals.

2 Samuel 6:5

I confess that there are some things you write about with the benefit of experience and practice. But sometimes you write because you look back and say, "Wow, I might have done better!" And sometimes you write about things because your children taught you. This chapter is the latter.

In the Bible, there are seven major festivals that occur on an annual basis. They are: (1) Passover, (2) Unleavened Bread, (3) First Fruits, (4) Pentecost, (5) Feast of Trumpets, (6) Day of Atonement, and (7) Feast of Booths.[1] These festivals were times of celebration. People took time off work. They broke away from their normal schedule. They took time to remember what God had done. They gave—they made offerings and sacrifices.

Passover began with a time of storytelling, where parents retold their children the story of God bringing them out of Egypt (Exod. 12:26–27). The Feast of Booths also included a practice of remembering. During the feast, the people were supposed to move out of their houses and live in tents or a booth so they could remember what it was like for Israel wandering in the wilderness.

As our family wrote out a vision, mission, and values, we committed to a once-a-year celebration. In that celebration we could renew our commitment to our vision, mission, and values. Everyone in the family knows the time of year we'll meet, and they do their absolute best to be there.

Our kids planned the first several celebrations, and now our grandchildren are planning them. Each of the celebrations reflects their unique personalities. We've had some incredibly fun ones—everything from fireworks to bands, full spreads to simple meals. Perhaps one of the most fun ones occurred just recently. We visited the site of our very first store—a simple 1,200-square-foot setup. That little celebration reminded us of where we began, and we could pray in gratitude.

That's the idea of celebration. It is *not* just a big party. It's typically not combined with any other holidays. It's an intentional time when we focus on our family identity. We remind each other of our values and our history—where we came from. We also challenge each other about our future—where God is taking us.

That's my encouragement to you. Set a family celebration day. Break away from your normal routine. Break away from work. Have some great food, and remind yourself of your vision, mission, and values, where you've been and where you are going. It's powerful to celebrate. I learned the art of celebrating from my children.

O Lord, thank You for the power and the reminder of celebration. Like David, we can celebrate with all our might and remember Your goodness to us!

DAY 47

RELINQUISH *the* TITLE

> Yours, LORD, is the greatness and the power and the glory and the majesty and the splendor, for everything in heaven and earth is yours.
>
> 1 Chronicles 29:11

As we've already discussed, God is the owner of everything—our cars, our houses, our lands, our bank accounts, our stuff. There is nothing that exists that He does not own. But what are the consequences of that ownership? How does recognizing Him as the owner change our lives?

I often say that it's easy to say that God is the owner of everything, but it's a lot harder to do something about it. As Bill and I have hosted CEO events over the years, we've had a lot of people nod their heads in agreement—"Yes, God is the owner." But their behavior is no different than the rest of the world.

When we are the owners of our stuff, we use it for selfish means. We expect enjoyment and pleasure from what we have. As employees, we expect the best benefits and salaries. As business owners, we expect the big payday.

What does it mean that God is the owner? He has the right and title to everything we have. When I realized what it really meant that God owned my company, I pulled out a sheet of paper and wrote: "God, this is Your company, and I signed my name to it."

And that's my encouragement to everyone reading these words: *relinquish the title*. If you've ever sold a car, there comes the moment when you have to transfer the title. You have to write in the new owner's name, and then you have to sign your name indicating that you have transferred the title to the new owner.

Do the same with God the Father. Give back to Him what was already His—all that He's put in your hands. Take out that sheet of paper and make a list of everything you are giving to Him. Is there anything you are holding back? Is there any precious possession that you call yours? As you make your list, take a moment to write that you are steward and manager of these assets and that you'll use them for God's purposes.

After you complete your list, stop and pray. Then sign your name to the list. When I finally did more than acknowledge God's ownership, I experienced a freedom I've never had before. I didn't have the responsibility or the worries; I was free to be a good steward and trust the results to Him.

O Lord, I acknowledge Your ownership in more than just words—I relinquish the title. I give up everything that I consider mine, and I put it in Your hands. I want to be a good steward of everything You've put before me and use it all for Your glory.

DAY 48

WORKING *in* COMMUNITY

And let us consider how we may spur one another on toward love and good deeds, not giving up meeting together, as some are in the habit of doing, but encouraging one another—and all the more as you see the Day approaching.

Hebrews 10:24–25

When my wife Barbara was growing up, she went to a Baptist church. I grew up in a Pentecostal church. I'll joke with her from time to time that as a Pentecostal, I'm trying to get her saved again. On the other hand, because I'm a Pentecostal, I get saved every Wednesday, Sunday morning, and Sunday evening. Barbara tells me that is not enough!

All teasing aside, I grew up in the church. My parents were pastors, and we were there every time the doors opened. Now, I know that some pastors' kids resent that kind of experience. For us, there was a difference. We worked together.

Our churches were so small, we had to work together to pull off a church service. As a family, we also worked outside the church—sometimes it was picking cotton or walking beans (weeding rows of soybeans). Because our churches were small and the actual income was small if we didn't work together as a family, it meant that our ability to buy groceries, pay rent, buy shoes, and so on would all be limited. So we worked together.

I'm afraid for too many that church has become a place to be entertained instead of getting involved and working. Or worse, I've seen too many others back out of active church participation altogether. Instead, they focus on selecting their own community.

Part of the power of the local church is being with people who are different from you. When Paul talked about the idea of the different parts of the body in 1 Corinthians 12, he emphasized that we need each other. We need the young people to interact with their elders and vice versa. We need those with differing viewpoints to press established ways of thinking. We need those with a respect for the past and tradition to challenge those new ways of thinking. Those all make for a healthy body.

But when we self-select or choose not to participate, I'm afraid we err. Even today, our church is one that has a midweek service and two services on Sunday. I'm grateful for those and appreciate the opportunity to participate. It keeps me fresh and engaged, and it's something Barbara and I do together. We are working together for the building up of the body.

Where do you stand with your local body of believers? Are you engaged? Or are you entertained? Do you dig deep, shoulder to shoulder with a community of like-minded people? And do you continue to put yourself in the company of those who might disagree with you? Indeed, "let us consider how we may spur one another on toward love and good deeds, not giving up meeting together" (Heb. 10:24).

O Lord, thank You for this reminder that working together in the company of fellow believers stirs and stimulates me to follow You!

DAY 49

RISKY GENEROSITY

> In the midst of a very severe trial, their overflowing joy and their extreme poverty welled up in rich generosity. For I testify that they gave as much as they were able, and even beyond their ability.
>
> 2 Corinthians 8:2–3

I'm not sure what was going on in the Macedonian church when Paul wrote those words. All we know is that they faced a severe trial and extreme poverty. Yet during this trial and poverty, they were generous—even beyond what seemed possible.

In fact, in verse four from this same passage, Paul says they urgently pleaded for the opportunity to be generous. They wanted to help others. You could've made the argument that it was the Macedonian church that needed help!

I remember hearing from a man not long ago that in the early days of his business, he was challenged by

God to give out of his profit. If you know business startups, things are lean in the beginning. There's just not a lot of margin for error. It's far easier to say that you'll give when you have more profit, when you've got more excess. But there it was: He'd finally gotten over the hump where income was greater than expenses, and he showed a profit of $16.00. He wrote a check for $1.60 and has never looked back.

The Macedonian church practiced risky generosity. A check for $1.60 represents risky generosity. Sometimes people ask me how much they should give. Maybe they've got young families, mortgages to cover, and college costs that are coming. Or maybe they've got businesses in full-on growth mode—it takes cash to grow a business. They ask a simple question: How do I grow a business and still give or stretch my giving?

I can't give them a formula. I just know that if our giving doesn't test us in some way, then we may not be where we need to be. There should be some tension in our generosity. If there's not some want, desire, or even some necessity that is put on hold, then maybe we need to rethink our giving. Or perhaps we're facing some opportunity for expansion, some new market to open, some new ministry to be added. If there isn't some need for pause, then maybe our generosity is not risky enough.

When Abraham took Isaac to the mountain to be sacrificed, he surely faced tension over the sacrifice that he was going to make. The apostle Paul was constantly in tension over giving his life away for the gospel. Even Jesus, in the moment of His greatest sacrifice, asked the Father if there was another way.

When my generosity is risky, when there's some tension in it, I think I can be assured that I'm on the right path for living a powerful legacy.

O Lord, help me to pause in reflection. Am I comfortable in my giving? Or am I in a place where it causes me tension and challenges my lifestyle in some way? In that place, I experience Your joy.

DAY 50

WHAT ARE YOUR LEGACY SYMBOLS?

> Early the next morning Jacob took the stone he had placed under his head and set it up as a pillar and poured oil on top of it. He called that place Bethel, though the city used to be called Luz.
>
> Genesis 28:18–19

There's this thing about stones in Scripture. Jacob, after hearing from God in a dream, took the stone he'd used for a pillow and set it up as a pillar. The stone stood as a symbol of the place where God met him. Later, in Genesis 31, after having a dispute, Jacob and Laban set up a pile of stones—a witness to the resolution of their disputes. Or when Israel crossed the Jordan to the promised land, in Joshua 4, they were to set up an altar of stones with the Ten Commandments written upon it. The altar was a symbol of mercy and grace.

What Are Your Legacy Symbols?

But it's not just about stones. There are lots of other symbols in the Bible:

- the rainbow—a symbol of God's mercy (Gen. 9:13)
- thunder, lightning, clouds, and smoke—a symbol of God's presence (Exod. 19:16–18)
- a throne—a symbol of God's glory (Isa. 6:1)
- fire—a symbol of the Holy Spirit (Acts 2:3)
- a signet ring—a symbol of authority (Esther 8:10)
- a banner or flag—a symbol of celebration or a rallying point (Ps. 20:5)
- the cross—a symbol of sacrifice (Luke 23:33)
- the color white—a symbol of purity (Rev. 3:4–5)

The list could go on and on! Why all the symbols? Symbols stand for something. They represent something. For instance, an army in the midst of battle could always look for their flag and rally there. They knew that wherever the flag was raised, they had fellow soldiers engaged in battle.

As families, we need our own symbols. Symbols help us remember. They are visual reminders of our identity. That's why in our family, we have our vision, mission, and values dressed up in a special document that everyone has. We also have a unique coin that has our vision and mission on it and a one-of-a-kind Bible that has a picture of the world on it. These are symbols of our family.

Sometimes we encourage families to develop their own family crest. The crest was a symbol with unique colors, animals, a flag, and a motto that represented the family and what it stood for. We've seen families pass on things like sourdough starters, watches, furniture, Bibles, songs, and musical instruments.

What are your family symbols? What will you pass on to your children that will be their artifacts of culture? Those symbols and artifacts are family identity visually represented.

O Lord, thank You for the power of Your Word and how You use symbols to remind us of Your presence. Help me to use symbols in my own life and the life of my family.

DAY 51

ARCHITECT YOUR PLAN

> Suppose one of you wants to build a tower. Won't you first sit down and estimate the cost to see if you have enough money to complete it?
>
> Luke 14:28

While I've never really used a mobile phone, my wife Barbara uses one all the time. When we travel out of town, she'll pull out her phone, type an address into the navigation app, and use it to help us get to where we are going. It's pretty handy. But in all the times we've used that app, we've never typed in "not sure" or "uncertain" and asked for directions. Even if we did, the phone wouldn't know what to do with those instructions.

I wonder if most of us live our lives that way—with no clear sense of direction or purpose. We are like feathers floating in the wind, waiting for direction. But as I look at the Bible, it seems to me that God's given us a very clear path for our lives. He wants us to have a clear vision, mission, and values for our lives.

If you walk into most companies, churches, and non-profits today, you'll typically see that they have a vision, mission, and values statement on display. They've often spent thousands of dollars on consultants to help them carefully craft these statements. Some go even further and hire chief culture officers to make sure these statements get integrated into the life of the organization.

But there's the simple question that if we spend all this time and money on architecture for our organizations, why don't we do the same for our families?

As we've discussed in previous devotions, vision is the idea of setting a clear picture and goal for the future. A mission statement is practical instruction on a day-by-day basis. It's the simple instruction we want to have for our own lives and for our children. Values are like the compass settings that provide guidance to the decisions we need to make in life.

Defining and writing down your vision, mission, and values is like writing down the blueprints for your life. That's why Luke was careful to record the instructions of Jesus. Carefully consider what kind of house you are trying to build. Do you have a blueprint? Do you have a plan to execute the blueprint?

It takes intentionality to live this way. One of the young men who came to one of our CEO events talked about his thirty-year plan for his life and for his children. Ultimately, he was planning for a multigenerational vision. The key is that he sat down and thought about it. He has written it down. He has got it plugged into his navigation app, and his chance of success is far greater than the average person's. What about you? Do you have your architecture in place?

O Lord, I'll admit that I've often been far more intentional about my work and professional life than I am about my family. Help me to put the architecture in place with Your guidance for a multigenerational vision.

DAY 52

WHAT'S YOUR CONDUCT CODE?

The LORD said to Moses, "Come up to me on the mountain and stay here, and I will give you the tablets of stone with the law and commandments I have written for their instruction."

Exodus 24:12

The Old Testament gets a bad rap. For many they might see it as a set of rules that don't apply to today.

But we need to take a step back. What's the purpose of the Old Testament, and, specifically, what's the purpose of all the laws? Weren't they just a set of rules put in place so that God could spank the children of Israel when they broke them?

The laws were really about giving the Israelites a code of conduct—a way of life—that was different from the rest of the world around them. Jesus, for instance, boiled down the Ten Commandments to two things: love God and love your neighbor as yourself. Speaking on the latter, he said in John 13:35, "By this everyone will know that you are my disciples, if you love one another."

The law—the code—was really about encouraging the Israelites to live differently than the rest of the world. By doing so, they would point people to the one God, the redeemer of our souls.

What's your code of conduct? John Wooden, the legendary basketball coach, tells how when he graduated from elementary school, his father gave him seven rules by which to live. They are: (1) Be true to yourself; (2) Help others; (3) Make each day your masterpiece; (4) Drink deeply from good books, especially the Bible; (5) Make friendship a fine art; (6) Build a shelter against a rainy day; and (7) Pray for guidance and count and give thanks for your blessings every day. This code or creed guided John throughout his life.[1]

This idea of having a code of conduct or creed is one of the simple ideas that helps us build a life of eternal significance. Your own rules of behavior—how you treat others—are key to an effective code. Some of those basic ideas are the commitment to love, the commitment to not gossip, the commitment to handle conflict, and the commitment to confess our sins and ask for forgiveness.

Romans 12:9–21 provides a great list of a way to live: "Love must be sincere. Hate what is evil; cling to what is good" (v. 9). Just like our vision, mission, and values, however, if a creed is not written down, then we end up with a situational code. Take the time to write down your code, your creed, your guiding principles, your rules of behavior.

O Lord, we love that You are a God who doesn't call us to wander but who wants us to live with a clear code of conduct, a way of life that distinguishes us from the rest of the world.

DAY 53

THE FREEDOM *of* STEWARDSHIP

> This, then, is how you ought to regard us: as servants of Christ.
>
> 1 Corinthians 4:1

There's one thousand problems with ownership. There is only one question and responsibility when it comes to stewardship. Hold that thought for a moment.

In the Corinthian church, there was a real problem of comparison. Some people viewed themselves as followers of Apollos, Cephas, Paul, or Christ (1 Cor. 1:12). In 1 Corinthians 4:1, Paul wanted to set the record straight: regard us as servants (or stewards) of Christ. By repositioning himself and other leaders as servants or stewards, they did not have to vie for favoritism or the following of a particular group.

Or consider my ownership of Hobby Lobby. As an owner, I always had to consider the risks of doing business—whether anyone was going to sue us, or if storms would force us to close stores. There was a host of things I had to think about: Are we going to be profitable? Do we have enough sales? Are our expenses in line? Do we have the right people? Do we have the right products?

The same issues apply in life, whether you own a business or not. Teachers, lawyers, customer service workers, mechanics, welders, pilots—the issues are the same. As owners, we become responsible for the results. We become responsible for mistakes. We take it upon ourselves.

With stewardship comes freedom. Back in 1 Corinthians, Paul said it this way: one plants, one waters, but "God has been making it grow" (1 Cor. 3:6).

In A. W. Tozer's *The Pursuit of God*, he describes the great struggle Abraham must've faced when God called him to sacrifice Isaac. A thousand questions must have flooded his mind. *How could God fulfill his blessing without a son? Surely by now he and Sarah would be too old to have another child.* It must've been a sleepless night.

After a long night of wrestling, Abraham finally decided to trust God. He made the long trek up the mountain and even took a knife in hand to slay his son before God stopped him. Abraham gave up ownership of his son to God. Tozer describes it so well: "He had everything, but he possessed nothing."[1]

That's the freedom of stewardship. When we possess nothing, we are free to let go. There is nothing that possesses our heart but God. When we own nothing, there are no dangerous tentacles of greed or covetousness that might find root in our heart.

What is the one responsibility of stewardship? Faithfulness. Be faithful and leave the results up to Him.

O Lord, may I experience the freedom of stewardship. May I experience the blessedness of possessing nothing.

DAY 54

THE IMPORTANCE *of* DISCIPLINE

> No discipline seems pleasant at the time, but painful. Later on, however, it produces a harvest of righteousness and peace for those who have been trained by it.
>
> Hebrews 12:11

Great legacies are not built overnight.

Sometimes people ask me when I knew Hobby Lobby was a success. That's not an easy question. When we started in 1970, we were working out of our garage. Our first store was a mere six hundred square feet of retail space and six hundred of inventory. We later graduated to five thousand square feet. When we had twelve or thirteen stores, we nearly went bankrupt. By 1997, we'd been named the Ernst & Young Entrepreneur of the Year in Retail. But even then, we didn't feel successful.

The Importance of Discipline

Now, here we are, fifty years later, with over one thousand stores, and we have the benefit of hindsight. That hindsight teaches us that we grew steadily and surely over a fifty-year period. There was no "Easy Button" and no major spike in sales. We exercised discipline one day at a time to be the best retailer.

I'm not sure there's a more challenging word in the English language than *discipline*. Webster's Dictionary defines it as "training that corrects, molds, or perfects the mental faculties or moral character."[1] At its heart, discipline is training. You can see the word *disciple* rooted there.

The writer of Hebrews said it well: Discipline is not pleasant. It's painful. It means changing from the way we are to the way we want to be. And the results typically are not immediate. In my own life, for years and years I loved the fizzy goodness of a Dr. Pepper, but over time I found that the sugar created inflammation in my joints. I had to train myself to stop asking for that drink at restaurants or when I wanted a pick-me-up during the day. It wasn't easy.

On the other hand, the Scriptures teach us the consequences of a lack of discipline. Proverbs 13:18 says, "Whoever disregards discipline comes to poverty and shame, but whoever heeds correction is honored."

Proverbs 10:17 points out the positive: "Whoever heeds discipline shows the way to life." Proverbs 5:23 says it bluntly: "For lack of discipline they will die."

What about you? How are your disciplines? In God's Word, in prayer, in fellowship, in your daily habits, in your thought life, in your attention to your marriage and your family? I've heard it said that discipline is the idea of long obedience in the same direction. Those who get distracted, who chase after shiny things or temporary affections and lusts, will not and cannot build lasting legacies.

O Lord, may my life be a long obedience in the same direction. May my life be marked by the daily discipline of becoming more conformed to Your image.

DAY 55

LEGACY PRACTICES—NOT

Kish had a son named Saul, as handsome a young man as could be found anywhere in Israel, and he was a head taller than anyone else.

1 Samuel 9:2

When I read about the life of King Saul, I'm saddened. His story unfolds from 1 Samuel 9 through 28—that's a lot of Bible real estate devoted to one person. His promise and potential were off the charts. As the first king of Israel, he was expected to reign over the people and to bring peace to the land (1 Sam. 10:1). If he'd been faithful, he might have had an enduring kingdom (1 Sam. 13:13), and we even see him prophesying (1 Sam. 10:10).

But that's about as good as it gets with Saul. His life is a sad story of a man who chose a different legacy. At the beginning of his story, he was described as a tall, handsome man not once but twice (1 Sam. 9:2). Absent from his description is anything related to his character. On top of that, he had literally lost his father's donkeys. While in pursuit, he was ready to give up (1 Sam. 9:5), which is unfortunately a trait he displayed throughout the rest of his life.

When it was time to assume the throne, we find him hiding among the baggage. From there, we see King Saul take shortcuts. Despite being told to wait seven days for Samuel to come and make the offering before battle, Saul assumed the role of priest and prophet and made the offering himself. Despite being told to get rid of the evil of the Amalekites, Saul spared the best of the resources for himself and the people. In each instance, he blamed his shortcomings on others. Saul never once seemed to take ownership for his own sin.

When it came to battle, his son Jonathan was the stronger leader. When it came to face Goliath, Saul let David, a teenager, lead the battle. When David got accolades, Saul became jealous and vengeful. He tried to use his own family against his rival. His pursuit to kill David lasted years.

Despite all these shortcomings, if Saul would have repented, if he would have acknowledged his sin, he might have had a different result. But instead, his legacy was marked by shortcuts, a failure to persist, disobedience, a lack of courage, a lack of repentance, taking the authority of others, selfish desires, revenge, and shifting blame. Saul's life is a recipe for how not to live in any facet of your life.

When we look at Saul's life, we should examine our own life with a similar lens. Am I taking shortcuts? Taking authority where I shouldn't? Where do I need to exhibit courage? What about repentance for my sin? Do I demonstrate only partial obedience? Do I celebrate the victories of others? Or do I pursue a course of revenge and shifting blame?

O Lord, these are hard lessons from the life of King Saul. Help me examine my life through Your Spirit so that I might be moved to a place of unconditional obedience and devotion.

DAY 56

A LEGACY *of* REPENTANCE

> After removing Saul, he made David their king. God testified concerning him: "I have found David son of Jesse, a man after my own heart; he will do everything I want him to do."
>
> Acts 13:22

King Saul and King David might be a study in contrasts. Saul was a tall, handsome man who stood out in a crowd; when Samuel was looking for the next king in Jesse's sons, no one thought to call David, the youngest child. When we first find Saul, he had lost his father's donkeys; David was keeping his father's sheep. Saul made an unauthorized offering in place of Samuel; David refused to take the life of Saul, the Lord's anointed. Saul was in the background while Goliath taunted Israel; David rushed to the front of the battle. Perhaps there's no greater compliment paid to David than the fact he was called a man after God's heart.

What can we learn from the practices of David? First and foremost, we see in David a heart of worship. As he writes in Psalm 63, he was a man who thirsted after God. That same psalm says that David took the time to behold God's glory, that he promised to offer praise "as long as I live," and that he lifted his hands in worship (Ps. 63:4). He remembered God in the "watches of the night" (Ps. 63:6). But we also see David as a leader of men, a warrior. He was a generous man. He led the way in funding the temple construction. In 1 Chronicles 29:2, David said, "With all my resources I have provided for the temple of my God."

Like Saul, David wasn't perfect. In fact, you could argue that his track record was just as troubled. He committed adultery and tried to cover it up. When his initial attempts didn't work, he committed murder. His family was a mess. One of his sons raped his daughter, and David did nothing. That rape led to murder by another of David's sons, and David again did nothing. Ultimately, his kingdom was put at risk by a conspiracy of one of his own sons.

What's the difference? When confronted by his own sin, David repented. Psalm 51 is David's heartfelt psalm of repentance. The cry of David's heart to "wash away all my iniquity" and to "create in me a pure heart, O God" has provided instruction for many wrestling with their own sin (Ps. 51:2, 10). David's brokenness over his sin is a repeated theme throughout his life.

Not perfection. Just repentance. That's the big difference between Saul and David. That message of repentance is a powerful call to us to examine our own lives in light of the holiness of God; to confront our sin; and then to own it, confess it, and turn from it. That's David's pursuit of God.

O Lord, thank You for reminding us that Saul and David were not that different—both were flawed men. But David repented of his sin. Help me to examine my life in view of Your own glory and to turn from my sin. Create in me a clean heart, O God, and renew a steadfast spirit in me!

DAY 57

KNOW YOUR STORY

This, then, is the family line of Perez: Perez was the father of Hezron, Hezron the father of Ram, Ram the father of Amminadab, Amminadab the father of Nahshon, Nahshon the father of Salmon, Salmon the father of Boaz, Boaz the father of Obed, Obed the father of Jesse, and Jesse the father of David.

Ruth 4:18–22

In 2022, Ancestry released the results of a survey showing that 53 percent of Americans could not name all four of their grandparents.[1] There used to be a time when family history meant something. I'm afraid today we've devalued the place of family genealogy and family history.

Years ago, it used to be that someone's favorite TV show might be something like *The Adventures of Ozzie and Harriet*, which featured a real-life family, or *My Three Sons*, which was about a widower raising his three sons. Then in the late 1980s, *Seinfeld*, a show about nothing, became popular. Five years after that, *Friends*, a show about a group of friends largely alienated from their own families and becoming their own family, came onto the scene. Still more recently, *Modern Family* showcased differing family types.

Though I don't know much about my ancestry, my great-grandchildren now have four generations to look back to: their parents, grandparents, myself and Barbara, and my parents. And because I know Bill's story, I know that he's named after his great-grandfather who was a moonshiner in the hills of the Missouri Ozarks. His own father was one of eight, living in a three-room log cabin in those same Ozarks.

We all come from a story. Some of those stories are admittedly not good. But the good and the bad are still our story. We can't change the past, but we can own it, acknowledge it, and pull lessons from it. We are not islands—people born as individuals and living our own destiny. We are always connected to a greater story.

We do the book of Ruth a disservice to read it and see Boaz as a man of standing, a man who stands on his own. Boaz, in keeping with the legacy definition, puts into motion a great legacy. He fathers Obed, who fathers Jesse, who fathers David, the great king of

Israel. Looking back, we know that Boaz comes from the line of Perez, who was born of questionable circumstances, in which his father was also his mom's father-in-law (see Genesis 38—more on that in a later devotion). Somehow, Perez overcame his tough start in life, and as far as we can tell, went on to live a life of great integrity.

We take the good and the bad of our story, and we move forward. As much as possible, we honor our parents, our grandparents, and even those who have long since passed. We tell their stories—what made them into the people they became. In so doing, we recognize that we are not alone. Our past informs us, even if it does not define us.

By connecting to our family's stories, we realize that we are part of a much bigger story—the redemption story of a great King who loves us enough to die for us.

O Lord, help me to understand my story, my past, for all the good and the bad, and to own that story so that I might help shape generations to come.

DAY 58

STUDY, STUDY, STUDY

> Keep this Book of the Law always on your lips; meditate on it day and night, so that you may be careful to do everything written in it. Then you will be prosperous and successful.
>
> Joshua 1:8

Sometimes Bill tells me that I geek out—on ribbons, or pony beads, or glue, or picture frames. I wake up every day ready to go into work. Hobby Lobby carries over eighty thousand items in our stores. Things are always changing.

Often, when we host a group of CEOs in our offices, we'll take a tour of our layout room, which is like a miniature Hobby Lobby. When I explain all the decisions that go into selling a product, I'll turn to one of the people in attendance and ask them to be the snowman buyer, for instance. They'll always agree.

Then I'll ask them to make the decision on how many snowmen we need to buy for the upcoming Christmas season. I tell them that our snowmen come in sizes ranging from three inches to thirty-six inches, eight different mediums, and a variety of colors and accessories. And they must come up with how many we'll buy. It's impossible.

Unless you study, study, study. What do I mean by that? In our case, it means that you study the products, study the colors, study the sizes. There's little doubt that, even with all of that, you'll still have to make educated guesses. But if you keep the mindset that you are going to keep studying, those decisions will get easier and easier.

That's why I love my work. The more I study, the more fun it gets. The more I study, the bigger a difference I can make. The bigger a difference I can make, the more money we make and the more we can tell people about Jesus. I think this principle applies no matter what job you have, no matter what industry you are in.

Are you bored in your work? I'll confess that a number of years ago, I was beginning to get bored. We'd hired such great people that I felt like the company could run on autopilot. At one level, I'd been doing retail for fifty years, so you might have been able to say I had it figured out. I didn't want to be bored. So, I asked God to give me something big to do. He directed me to begin studying and studying and studying new ways to market our merchandise. It was almost as if I was relearning the business again. It was so exciting.

That's my encouragement to you. Keep the heart of a lifelong learner in every aspect of your life. Work. Family. Marriage. Even if there's an area of your life you think you have figured out, there's always more. You can study and become better. You can always learn more. And when you keep that attitude of learning and growing, your life stays exciting. Study. Study. Study.

O Lord, give me a heart like Ezra who set his heart to study the Law of the Lord. Give me a heart to study in all areas of my life, so that I might remain diligent and excited in everything that I'm doing.

DAY 59

START WHERE YOU ARE

> I was cupbearer to the king.
> Nehemiah 1:11

It almost doesn't qualify as a verse. It's like an add-on. *I was cupbearer to the king.* While it's true that a cupbearer was a position of trust, what does it qualify you to do? Marshall resources? Build a team, rally a team, fight off the enemy, architect a plan, execute a plan, and build a wall within fifty-two days? I don't think so.

But what was the one thing Nehemiah had? He had access to the king. Even with the access, Nehemiah didn't abuse it. He took his burdens for Jerusalem and its ruined state to the Lord in prayer. He could start there.

From there, Nehemiah trusted God for results. It was the king who noticed Nehemiah's sadness and initiated help, resources, and favor for Nehemiah's mission. The Scriptures don't provide any insight on whether Nehemiah felt qualified or overwhelmed by the task at hand.

What we do know is that Nehemiah started with what he had. Even upon arriving in Jerusalem, he assessed the problem and rallied everyone to begin building. The message of Nehemiah is for everyone.

When Nehemiah received the news of Jerusalem's ruined state, he could have whined and moaned and done nothing about it but complain. He could have stopped there. We might be tempted to do the same when we think of our own legacy. Maybe there's been too much water under the bridge, too much hurt and pain, too much that seems off course.

We should take heart. We can have the greatest blueprint in the world for the most beautiful building, and we'll still have to make course corrections. We'll always have to adjust. There may even be times, like Nehemiah, when we come to a place where it seems like all is ruined. But, friend, let me tell you that *we are all cupbearers to the King*!

We all have access to the King of Kings and the Lord of Lords! We have access to the One who can restore every broken place, the One who can build up the ruins and rally the troops. We can trust that restoration to His care.

The future may hold good news, or it might hold pain. We can never know for sure. Even Nehemiah would not have been able to look ahead and see that Israel would be conquered again one day. But neither could he see that Israel would one day become a nation state in 1948. So keep believing. Keep praying, and start where you are.

O Lord, I come, and I bring my life, and I bring my family—all of them—to You. I pray that You'll build up every broken place, that You'll bring restoration and make something beautiful for generations to come.

DAY 60

RELENTLESS GRACE

Then the word of the LORD came to Jonah a second time: "Go to the great city of Nineveh and proclaim to it the message I give you."

Jonah 3:1–2

As you read these devotions and particularly these legacy practices, it would be easy to kick yourself. If you've got adult children, you might think, *It's too late for me*. The toothpaste is out of the tube.

Or it might be that, as you read these practices, you think, *Wow, I've done none of these*. Or maybe you're just trying to keep your life together, and this feels like just another to-do list.

Even for me, I write with the benefit of my coauthor, Bill's, help and wisdom. He works on the front line with families, and he's seen some of the best practices. I got some of these things right, but we were by no means perfect.

That's my encouragement to you: Hang in there. Do the best you can with what you have. So much of living this life, raising a family, and leading organizations, is about being faithful with what you've been given. God's grace covers the rest.

Think about Jonah. God gave him a call to go and preach to Nineveh. Jonah wasn't even faithful to obey that call. He ran the opposite way. God could've gotten another person to do the job. But He pursued Jonah. He sent a storm. The storm was so violent that the crew started throwing cargo overboard. And Jonah? He was oblivious. He was asleep belowdecks, unaware of a desperate crew trying to save their lives. When they woke him, Jonah was ready to give up—he told the crew to throw him into the sea. The crew tried harder. They made a mighty push toward land.

When all their efforts had failed, they pitched Jonah into the sea. Jonah thought his life was over. But God. The Scriptures tell us, "And the LORD appointed a great fish to swallow up Jonah" (Jon. 1:17 ESV). There in the belly of the fish, God met Jonah and reminded him, "Salvation belongs to the LORD" (Jon. 2:9 ESV).

That's the way God is. He pursues us. Even in our disobedience, His desire is for us to experience His great love over us. If God will pursue us even to the belly of a fish, how much more will He pursue us daily if we yield to Him? We don't have to have the perfect formula or the perfect schedule. He'll take all our weakness and all our imperfection, and He'll turn it into something really, really good.

That's the way of His relentless grace. Even in the case of Jonah, his mission was to tell Nineveh that because their lives were opposed to God, they were doomed for destruction. Upon receiving that message, they repented, and God's grace saved them.

O Lord, thank You! I want to live a Legacy Life, but I mess up. I don't do things right and even make them worse. Thank You for covering me with Your relentless grace.

PART III

The LEGACY ADVENTURE

DAY 61

FROM GENERATION *to* GENERATION

One generation commends your works to another;
they tell of your mighty acts.

Psalm 145:4

I always said that school was one of my worst subjects.

I can't say that I was particularly proud of that. My goal was to get out of high school as quickly as I could. So I took four classes my junior and senior year: Math, English, Distributive Education, and Work. I got out of school by 11 a.m. and was off to work, and I got credit for working—while getting paid! I thought that was a great deal.

One class I didn't take was history. History is one of those things you don't appreciate until you have a need to look back. Now that I'm in my eighties, I've got occasion to look back. I think back now to my mom and dad. Small congregations and a big family meant that finances were always tight. I remember my parents down on their knees crying out for God's provision. That image is frozen in my mind. It's their legacy of prayer.

When I think about Barbara and me, there are similar reminders of our own great need—the risk of starting a business with a young family. We later nearly lost the business to bankruptcy, and then there was the uncertainty of government fines that could have crippled us. More recently, it was the pandemic that found us walking around empty warehouses, asking God for a chance to get open again.

Our children and their spouses have walked with us in these times of trial. Now I see them living their own legacies of faith. I'm so proud of them: Mart and Diana for being champions of Bible translation. Steve and Jackie for being champions of the Museum of the Bible. Stan and Darsee for being great leaders in the company. I know that each of them has had their own trials, twists, and turns.

Now I see this same legacy of faith in their children. My grandchildren are risk-takers in their own rights. They've been willing to take on tall challenges, get involved in the trenches of people's lives, and work for systemic change not only in Oklahoma City but in the pro-life arena. I've seen them serve by fostering children and adopting children. Their journeys have not been without hardship, but still I see them carry on.

It continues with my great-grandchildren. While many of them are still young, I see them being raised in godly homes and carrying the same sweet spirit of their parents. I'm not sure where they will land—maybe they'll be artists, singers, soccer players, lawyers, doctors, or, yes, maybe some will choose to be part of the family business.

But most of all, it is the legacy of faith that I care about. One generation telling of His works to the next. We are five generations in—may they keep the story going.

O Lord, may we all aspire to be a family telling Your good story from generation to generation.

DAY 62

LEGACY WEAVING

> In his defense Jesus said to them, "My Father is always at his work to this very day, and I too am working."
>
> John 5:17

The Father is always working. That's a big statement. And it's the cause for a particularly big admission. *He's working even if we don't see it.* Let me share the story of my coauthor, Bill. Like me, he grew up extremely poor. We kid about who grew up poorer! His family was on and off welfare and just barely made ends meet. A house fire destroyed their rental house and forced a move to Waldron, Missouri, a town of a hundred people along the banks of the Missouri River. Years later, that house fire would prove to be the best thing that ever happened to him, but at the time it seemed like the lowest period of his life.

Bill's neighbors from two houses down had become Christians through a little church plant there in

Legacy Weaving

Waldron. They brought Bill and his family a children's Bible storybook. Bill read that thing from cover to cover. For the first time, he heard the stories of Abraham and Isaac, Moses and the deliverance of Israel, and Joshua and the battle of Jericho, and he heard about Jesus. The neighbors invited him to church, and there in that little church Bill gave his life to Christ. It was the beginning of his own Legacy Life.

For a long time, that's all Bill knew of the story. But by chance, Bill reached out to one of the families who was part of that little church plant in Waldron. That's where he learned the rest of the story.

Three families who had been part of a much larger suburban church had decided that God had put it on their hearts to plant a church in Waldron, Missouri. (Think about it—who plants a church in a town of one hundred? What kind of return on investment comes from that?) The little church plant hired an intern from the local seminary to deliver messages on Sunday. Those three families labored away in that little community. They found a small house to rent for Sunday services. As it turns out, some of the first converts were Bill's neighbors—the very same neighbors who later brought him a children's Bible storybook.

The house fire was a bad day. It forced a move to a little nothing town and a really bad house. And there in that little town, Bill's dad would die of cancer. But on that bad day, God was legacy-weaving.

In that town of one hundred people, someone decided to plant a church where it didn't make sense to. They labored for only a handful of converts, but two of those converts shared their faith with Bill. That little act of obedience set in motion a great legacy for Bill and his family. So, if you are despairing in this moment, remember that "My Father is always at his work," even if we don't see it (John 5:17).

O Lord, we thank You that You are weaving a wonderful legacy—even if we don't see how all the threads are coming together.

DAY 63

FOURTEEN HUNDRED YEARS *of* FAMILY

> Then we your people, the sheep of your pasture, will praise you forever; from generation to generation we will proclaim your praise.
>
> Psalm 79:13

What's the oldest family-owned business in the world? One hundred years old, two hundred years old? Try fourteen hundred years! In AD 578, Prince Shōtoku Taishi commissioned construction of the first Japanese Buddhist temple. Shigetsu Kongō was part of that first temple build, and as Buddhism grew in Japan in the coming years, so did his construction business, Kongō Gumi. Temple building proved to be a steady source of income since temples frequently faced damage from natural disasters and wars.

The family was careful to preserve the secrets to building temples. The thirty-second head of the company, Yoshisada Kongō, documented the family creed. The creed consisted of sixteen principles designed to guide and preserve the family business into the future. Their creed is more than just a guide for the business but also a guide for their family. It contains principles on how to dress, how much to drink, and how to treat others. And at the forefront of the family's creed? Faith. In their case, the family focused on the tenets of Confucianism, Buddhism, and Shinto.

New workers were expected to undergo ten years of apprenticeship and another ten years of training to earn the distinction of master carpenter. Despite being guided by tradition, the family was wise enough to recognize the power of flexibility in adapting to changing times. They were one of the first to utilize concrete in wooden temples as well as computer-aided design programs for temple construction.

Most of all, they recognized the power of being led by family. However, even that tradition was challenged. When one generation produced no sons worthy of leadership, the family adopted a son-in-law who took on the Kongō name. In another case, when the male leader committed ritual suicide because of his failure to help the company thrive, his widow took over and admirably led the company to a new era.

In 2006 as temple revenues decreased and real estate values plummeted, Kongō Gumi was acquired by a private equity company. Today, it operates as a division of a much larger company. But for over fourteen hundred years it stood the test of time. Still, twice a month—on the first and fifteenth—Kongō Gumi workers gather for prayers of gratitude for their great history.[1]

In our microwave, instant-oatmeal world, it's hard to believe that a family business might survive for fifty generations. But the Kongō Gumi story stands as a great testimony to a family willing to live by a creed, to choose patience over immediate gratification, and to honor tradition while respecting the need to change. And while not a story of Christian faith, they truly represent the idea of carrying vision, mission, and values from generation to generation.

O Lord, we are reminded that all truth is Your truth, and in the story of Kongō Gumi we are reminded that we ought to set our sights higher and longer for generational influence and impact.

DAY 64

FOR *a* THOUSAND GENERATIONS

But showing love to a thousand generations of those who love me and keep my commandments.

Exodus 20:6

It's hard to think long-term when you are only 250 years old.

When I was graduating from high school, it was hard for me to think past military service, getting my first job, getting married, and having a family. But there is another way. Across the pond, as they say, the roots of family run deep. America is only about 250 years old, so we don't have that same appreciation.

Here in America, when we think about building something, we usually think about twenty years, maybe thirty. There are few of us who will pass down houses for generations. We may build and eventually we'll sell. Maybe we'll downsize. Maybe we'll end up in a facility for seniors. I can't say I like that thought. But it used to be that as family aged, they moved in with other family.

Similarly, in America, if you have a business, you build it to sell it. The sale is the time when you can capitalize on all your hard work and retire. Play golf, maybe. And if you decide to pass a business on to your children, well, we've seen plenty of examples of that not going well.

But let me give you a sampling of family businesses that lasted far longer than most of us in America can imagine:

Hōshi Ryokan, Japan (hotel): since AD 718

Fonderia Pontificia Marinelli, Italy (bell foundry): since AD 1000

Hotel Pilgrim Haus, Germany (hotel): since AD 1304

Richard de Bas, France (paper production): since AD 1326

Camuffo, Italy (shipbuilding): since AD 1438

Fabbrica D'Armi Pietro Beretta S.p.A, Italy (firearms): since AD 1526

John Brooke & Sons, United Kingdom (woolens): since AD 1541

Codorniu, Spain (winery): since AD 1551
Fonjallaz, Switzerland (winery): since AD 1552
Kikkoman, Japan (soy sauce production): since AD 1630[1]

That of course is only a partial list. There are seventeen countries represented in the original list we've pulled these from. But just this short list should encourage us and challenge us. We should think about building families that will last a thousand generations.

O Lord, we love that You are a God of order, not of chaos. Your design is for things that last for thousands of generations. May we seek to follow this design in our families.

DAY 65

SON *of a* CYMBAL MAKER

Moreover, I have appointed Oholiab son of Ahisamak, of the tribe of Dan, to help him. Also I have given ability to all the skilled workers to make everything I have commanded you.

Exodus 31:6

In 1618, Avedis worked as a metalsmith for the sultan of the Ottoman Empire. Cymbals had existed for generations, but Avedis developed a unique alloy of tin, copper, and silver that strengthened the instrument so it would not shatter. In 1623, the sultan officially bestowed on Avedis the surname Zildjian, which meant "son of a cymbal maker." Avedis was allowed to leave the court of the sultan to start his own business.

For the next three hundred years, the business remained relatively small by all standards. The secret formula was passed from generation to generation.

Through the late nineteenth and early twentieth centuries, the cymbal-making efforts were led by Aram Zildjian. However, Aram sought a successor.[1]

He wrote to his nephew Avedis III, who had settled in Boston, Massachusetts, to take over. Avedis III initially refused, but eventually Aram moved to the United States. By 1929, a plant was up and running. About that time, jazz music was growing in popularity, and the Zildjians were on the forefront with their cymbals.

However, it was the rise of rock music that catapulted the company. In 1964, the Beatles appeared on *The Ed Sullivan Show*. Ringo Starr, the band's drummer, featured Zildjian cymbals. It was only a matter of time before the Zildjians had ninety thousand back orders.

Today, they continue to operate in Massachusetts—four hundred years and fourteen generations later, with a fifteenth generation in training.[2]

Like Oholiab in Exodus 31:6, the Zildjian family developed a unique skill and formula. They carefully guarded it and passed it down from generation to generation. Even today, there are parts of their plant visitors are not allowed to see in order to guard their secrets. For much of their history, they were a small business, but they possessed a unique skill.

It's a great lesson. We can pass on skills and knowledge from generation to generation. It might be metalsmithing, woodworking, bread baking, piano playing, or some other kind of skill. Our job is to carefully consider the skills, talents, and abilities we can pass to our children, grandchildren, and so on.

O Lord, thank You for providing each of us with unique skills, talents, and abilities. Please help us to select the skills You want us to pass from one generation to the next as a way to bring You glory.

DAY 66

THE SURPRISING PASTOR'S LEGACY

Those who are wise will shine like the brightness of the heavens, and those who lead many to righteousness, like the stars for ever and ever.

Daniel 12:3

Perhaps you've heard of the incredible ministry of Jonathan Edwards.

Sometimes when we think of legacy, I'm afraid we think of it in terms of money and business. Not so with Edwards. He was born into the family of a preacher in 1703 in Connecticut. He died at the age of fifty-four.

In his short fifty-four years, Edwards's life reads like a movie script. He entered Yale College at thirteen and graduated around age seventeen. For two years, he studied divinity, took a brief pastorate, and had his master's degree by twenty. By his mid-twenties, he had become the pastor of the influential Northampton Church in Massachusetts. There he met his wife, Sarah Pierrepont, and together they had eleven children.

Edwards was renowned for his rigorous study. He rose at four in the morning with the goal of reading as much as thirteen hours a day. He lived with the simple aim of soli Deo gloria—for the glory of God alone. Edwards saw ample growth not only in the size of his congregation but in the depth of their devotion to Christ. He delivered a series of sermons on justification by faith alone that led to a great revival in the Connecticut River valley. He was part of the Great Awakening in 1740–1742, and his numerous essays helped shape a proper theology of those activities.[1]

Edwards's influence remained strong for another two centuries after his death. Today, scholars still turn to Edwards for help in understanding the issues of the present day.

But for all his work in the church, perhaps Edwards's greatest work was in his own family. In 1900, A.E. Winship published a book about Edwards and his family legacy. Winship compared the Edwards legacy to that of another man of the same era, Max Jukes.

Winship noted that the Edwards family counted among their number one US vice president (Aaron

Burr), one dean of a law school, one dean of a medical school, three US senators, three governors, three mayors, thirteen college presidents, thirty judges, sixty doctors, sixty-five professors, seventy-five military officers, eighty public office holders, one hundred lawyers, one hundred clergymen, and 285 college graduates.

Jukes, on the other hand, was a convict who counted among his descendants seven murderers, fifty prostitutes, sixty thieves, 130 other convicts, 310 paupers, and four hundred men and women who were "physically wrecked by their own wickedness."[2] What a difference in the legacies of those who follow Christ and those who do not.

O Lord, may I live a great spiritual legacy—soli Deo gloria. And in so doing, may my life affect the generations to come for Your glory alone.

DAY 67

THE JANITOR'S LEGACY

> The King will reply, "Truly I tell you, whatever you did for one of the least of these brothers and sisters of mine, you did for me."
>
> Matthew 25:40

Great legacies take place on and off the stage. Big Mike was never a guy for the stage. In fact, he was the school janitor. Mike Hill first met pastor Jim Bachmann while working for a school that was part of the church Bachmann had started. When Bachmann left to take on a new church assignment at Stephens Valley Church in Nashville, Tennessee, Hill joined that church. Bachmann described Hill as big, strong, tough, but also soft and tender.

Hill was always hugging on the kids, each and every one of them. His smile was infectious. Maybe that came from Hill's love for his own family; he had seven children and fourteen grandchildren. Hill's children told how every few days they could expect to receive a simple text message saying, "I love you."

Big Mike loved to cook, and sometimes he brought chocolate chip cookies for Bachmann. For a special occasion he might even bring a pecan or chess pie. Bachmann joked, "He led me into temptation. He did not deliver me from it."[1]

One day, a gunman came into the school and shot three adults and three children. Hill was one of the victims. In the aftermath of the tragedy, Hill's own family called for compassion for everyone involved.[2]

At Big Mike's funeral, hundreds turned out to honor his life and memory. A fundraiser was set up in Hill's name and more than $600,000 was raised—well above the original $25,000 goal.

When I think of Mike Hill, I think about a great legacy. He didn't occupy a big platform, never wrote a book as far as I know, and not many would have recognized his name but for the tragedy. But Hill loved well the people who were within arm's reach. I love that thought: love well those within arm's reach.

I think that's some of what Jesus was saying in Matthew 25:40: "Whatever you did for the least of these brothers and sisters of mine, you did for me." The disciples of Jesus were often confused about the nature of Jesus's kingdom. And for good reason, I suppose. The world around them flaunted those who dressed better, lived in better houses, and sat upon thrones and commanded audiences.

The economy of Jesus lifted up those who lived a simpler way—the poor, the widow, the foreigner, the needy. That's the powerful lesson of the Legacy Life. It's a life that realizes that while legacy is forward-looking, it's also a life that seizes the moment. It serves and gives right now. It doesn't have to wait until there's a better day or a better moment.

O Lord, help me live today by loving those within arm's reach. Let me be generous with my hugs and my affirmations of love and kindness.

DAY 68

THE PASTOR'S WIFE

> For those who exalt themselves will be humbled, and those who humble themselves will be exalted.
>
> Matthew 23:12

What does your balance sheet look like?

A balance sheet is your listing of assets and liabilities. It's worth keeping in mind that the things the world counts are not those things that God counts.

My mother didn't have much of a balance sheet when she died. She didn't have much in the way of finances, and she depended on her family to take care of her. She had no big houses, caretakers, or assistants.

She was a pastor's wife, and although she'd preached her fair share of sermons, they never reached the masses. Most of the churches my parents pastored had a hundred people or fewer. Her closet was minimal. There were no glistening gowns or fancy shoes. The cupboard was largely bare.

In terms of a worldly financial statement, her balance was largely zero. Perhaps you might feel like my mom. Perhaps you might look around and compare yourself to others and say, "Wow, I haven't done much. I haven't accomplished much."

But take heart. My mom died in the arms of my sister. In her final breaths, she called out, "Do you see them? Do you see them?" Angels! Angels had come to take my mom home.

She was so rich, so wealthy in God's sight, that He sent angels to bring her to heaven. Her balance sheet was full. I've often said that any billionaire would trade places with my mom.

She'd cultivated a great heart, a great marriage, and a great family for Jesus. She'd set in motion a great legacy.

And don't miss this point: God's balance sheet is not completed just in this life. It's a generational balance sheet. We'll see the fruit of future generations that we've impacted, and the final accounting is never just in this moment, this time, and this equation.

Is it any wonder then that God says that those who humble themselves will be exalted?

O Lord, help me to be faithful and to realize that the results of the moment are different than the results that are written on the generational balance sheet.

DAY 69

IT'S NOT WHERE YOU BEGIN

Who dares despise the day of small things?
Zechariah 4:10

Perez didn't have a good start in this world. He was born to a single mom, and his father, Judah, was also his mom's father-in-law. His mom was first married to his grandfather's son, but that son died, and then his grandfather's second son married his mom, but *that* son also died. His mom was left single and vulnerable, so she disguised herself as a prostitute. Perez's father—his mom's father-in-law—came along and hired her, and that's how he came into the world.

Did you get all of that? Whew, it's complicated and messy. Can you imagine what would happen if the kids at school asked Perez about his parents? Or what about the awkward glances Perez's parents must have exchanged anytime the story of his birth came up?

Let's face it. It would be easy to complain and moan about such a messed-up family. But Perez didn't get stuck by his messy background. God's redemptive purposes were still at work, and He brought much good to the world through Perez's line. How do we know that?

You have to fast-forward about seven generations to the time of Ruth. Ruth marries Boaz. At the time of her marriage, the elders pronounce a blessing upon Boaz and Ruth:

> May you have standing in Ephrathah and be famous in Bethlehem. Through the offspring the LORD gives you by this young woman, may your family be like that of Perez, whom Tamar bore to Judah. (Ruth 4:11–12)

Despite Perez's messy start, the elders are blessing the marriage and future generations *to be like the house of Perez*. What do we know about the house of Perez? Perez's grandson many generations over, Boaz, is described as a "man of standing" (Ruth 2:1).

Boaz and Ruth become the parents of Obed. Obed is the father of Jesse, and Jesse is the father of King David. Later, in 1 Chronicles 27:3, Jashobeam, a descendant of

Perez, is a commander in David's army. Ultimately, Jesus is a descendant of Perez. Somewhere along the line, and despite his very messed-up beginning, Perez chose a different way—a life of integrity. His life of integrity set in motion generations of faithfulness, leading to Jesus. No matter how we begin, we can make choices to live uprightly that will influence future generations.

O Lord, we thank You for the story of Perez. We thank You that, even though we may have rough beginnings, You give us the power to make right choices today that will change the direction of future generations.

DAY 70

THE LOSS *of the* WORLD'S GREATEST FORTUNE

What good will it be for someone to gain the whole world, yet forfeit their soul? Or what can anyone give in exchange for their soul?

Matthew 16:26

Cornelius Vanderbilt was the richest man in America in his time.[1] He quit school at age eleven to help his father in the ferry business, and by age sixteen, he'd started his own ferry business in the New York Harbor. Because of his energy and aggressiveness, the other ferry captains began calling him the Commodore, and the name stuck. By age twenty-three, Vanderbilt moved into the steamboat business. Starting regional, he expanded into ocean vessels and later transatlantic ships.

By the 1850s, Vanderbilt moved into running railroads and eventually sold his steamship business. He became dominant in the railroad business and was responsible for driving the construction of Grand Central Station in New York. At the time of his death in 1877, Vanderbilt was worth $100 million dollars—which made him the wealthiest man in America.[2] Today, that amount would be equivalent to a multibillion-dollar estate.

He left the bulk of his estate to his oldest son, William. At the time of his death, he had nine other living children, who ended up suing the estate. Ultimately, William settled with his siblings, which made each of them wealthy. William lived just eight years after his father, and by the third generation, the Vanderbilts had become a family living off inherited wealth.

They built the finest houses in New York. They had the best yachts, country homes, expensive European vacations—there was no excess they denied themselves. One of their homes, the Biltmore Estate in Asheville, North Carolina, was an astonishing 175,000 square feet. By the third generation, however, the wealth was no longer growing. In fact, as the spending continued into the fourth generation, the wealth was on the decline—even if they did not realize it.

By the fifth generation, much of the wealth was gone. Think about it. An entire multibillion-dollar fortune wasted in five generations. In 1973, when 120 of the Vanderbilts gathered for a reunion at Vanderbilt University, few of them were millionaires. The bulk of the wealth had been lost.

What caused the fall of the Vanderbilt family? We know that it wasn't a lack of financial resources. They had more than anyone in America, and they still failed. They proved true the verse "What good is it for someone to gain the whole world, yet forfeit their soul?" (Mark 8:36). If we measure our family wealth in only money, then we'll certainly never sustain it. We measure wealth in all forms: spiritual, emotional, intellectual, social, and financial capital.

O Lord, we are mindful that great financial wealth is easily lost. It comes and it goes, but the wealth that lasts to eternity is always spiritual capital. Help me to invest in that way for my life and into the lives of others.

DAY 71

THE ROTHSCHILD LEGACY

Like arrows in the hands of a warrior are children born in one's youth. Blessed is the man whose quiver is full of them.

Psalm 127:4–5

The Vanderbilts lost one of the greatest fortunes in the world. Similarly, the Rothschild family were contemporaries of the Vanderbilt family in Europe.

In 1744, Mayer Rothschild was born in Frankfurt, Germany. With a strong Jewish heritage, he grew up with a deep appreciation of family. His grandfather and father were small businessmen. Mayer was actually sent to rabbinical school, but when his parents died suddenly of illness, he was apprenticed in business. In time, he started his own business trading in coins, art, and collectibles. Over time, that work led to finance and banking.

He engaged his five sons in the business. Each of them was an active participant not only in Frankfurt but also in Paris, London, Vienna, and Naples. Mayer insisted upon strong communication among the brothers about their activities. This communication allowed them to learn from one another and take advantage of the various opportunities being presented to each of them.

They were by no means a perfect family or without challenges. From the external perspective, they lived in a time when Jews were looked down upon and often segregated in the cities in which they lived. From inside the family, Mayer was a typical controlling patriarch, prone to criticizing his children.

Notwithstanding those challenges, Mayer transitioned the business by 1810, with the name of business officially changed to Mayer Amschel Rothschild & Sons. As a central tenet, the family had three core values: unity, integrity, and industry. The family crest was a fist clutching five arrows. The crest was based upon Psalm 127:4–5.

As part of his biblical roots, Mayer and his sons were faithful givers; they gave a tenth of their proceeds to help the poor in their community. Notably, even as the business transitioned to the second generation, the five boys were careful to remind themselves of the values of their father. Mayer himself pointed out to his sons that Jewish wealth rarely lasted into a second generation.[1]

Today, the Rothschild family business continues. While privately held, their business spans multiple industries, including banking, finance, and insurance. Why did the Rothschilds succeed and the Vanderbilts fail? Certainly, one big difference is that the Rothschild family was marked by generosity, a clear set of values, and a commitment to communication.

> *O Lord, help me to ponder and give me insight on why some families succeed for generations and others fail. Help me then to take those steps that You impress on me that might impact even the generations that I'll never see.*

DAY 72

WHAT ARE YOUR DYING WISHES?

> Then he blessed Joseph and said ". . . the Angel who has delivered me from all harm—may he bless these boys. May they be called by my name and the names of my fathers Abraham and Isaac, and may they increase greatly on the earth."
>
> Genesis 48:15–16

I think your final moments on this earth are telling. In Genesis 48, Jacob's blessing on Joseph's sons is simple: he prays that they'll still be identified as God's children. He prays that they'll be true to the family lineage and that they'll increase greatly on the earth. It's a great last wish.

In the last two devotionals, I've talked about the Vanderbilt family and the Rothschild family. Cornelius Vanderbilt and Mayer Rothschild both had dying wishes—even if they were quite different.

Much of the final year of Cornelius's life was marked by ill health. Daily doctor's visits and even visits by spiritualists could not alleviate his fear of death. It didn't help that the newspapers reported on his daily health; it was going to be big news when the richest man in America died. Sometimes he broke out in fits of rage. He didn't allow any of his children to visit him—except for his oldest son, William. His dying wish to William was stern instruction: "Keep the money together!"

True to those wishes, the vast majority of the estate went to William. It's not surprising that, in the coming generations, the Vanderbilts were marked by great spending. New York mansions, summer homes, yachts, race cars—you name it, they had it.

Mayer Rothschild had similar health issues in his final days. Unlike Cornelius, no entourage followed his health updates. For much of his life, Mayer had stressed to his five sons the necessity of the unity of their relationships. He warned that Jewish fortunes typically don't keep longer than two generations. Mayer's deathbed instructions to his oldest son, Amschel, emphasized family, not money: "Amschel, keep your brothers together, and you will become the richest people in Germany."[1]

Two vast fortunes with two vastly different deathbed blessings—one with the emphasis on money, and the other with an emphasis on family. While the Rothschilds were not without family conflict, long after their father's death, the five Rothschild brothers continued to remind each other of their father's instruction to keep the family together. As author Niall Ferguson said, "The impressive thing about the Rothschilds, however, is that the sons heeded their father so zealously."[2]

O Lord, thank You for this instruction. May my aim in life and therefore my dying wish for my family be unity of heart, mind, and spirit, so they might be all they can be in Christ.

DAY 73

SOMETIMES YOU'LL NEVER KNOW

> After Jesus was born in Bethlehem in Judea, during the time of King Herod, Magi from the east came to Jerusalem and asked, "Where is the one who has been born king of the Jews? We saw his star when it rose and have come to worship him."
>
> Matthew 2:1–2

If you've ever sat through a Christmas play, it's likely that you've seen a trio of wise men enter the scene. They bring with them gifts of frankincense, myrrh, and gold. The Bible records that they came from the east. But it leaves open a lot of questions, like, Why did they know to look for a star? And why was it important to them?

There are lots of theories around the wise men. Many commentators on the passage believe that the wise men were the product of Daniel's legacy. In Daniel

5:11, we know, for instance, that he was appointed chief of the magi. We also know that he was a consistent and faithful witness.

Hugh Whelchel says, "The Magi of the first century would have most certainly studied the writing of Daniel. . . . This connection between Daniel and Magi *may* help to explain why the Magi in question 600 years later expected a Jewish king to arrive in Judea near the end of the first century."[1]

But notice the operative word—*may*. No one can really say for sure that Daniel is responsible for the Magi appearing on the scene. It's speculation, at least on this side of heaven. What we do know is that the Magi did appear. And we do know that Daniel was faithful. He did the right thing.

That's the way it is with legacy.

Sometimes—in fact, much of the time—you'll never really know the impact of your life. Daniel didn't know the impact of living faithful to God in a time of exile. He knew, however, that it was the right thing to do. He knew that he wouldn't defile himself with the king's rich foods. He knew that he'd continue to pray to God no matter what the king's edict was, and no matter what the consequences would be.

Doing the right thing for the right reason is always the right path to take. We know that Daniel's conduct had an impact on the king. We suspect that his faith and his teaching impacted others. We suspect he set a powerful legacy in motion. But in that day and in that time, Daniel simply didn't know what impact he might have on future generations.

So it is with us. Like Daniel, we live and act faithfully now in our own generation. We pray and believe the impact will be for generations to come.

O Lord, let me live faithfully, declaring Your purposes and Your name in my generation and trusting You for the results in future generations.

DAY 74

LEGACY THROUGH LOSS

Precious in the sight of the LORD is the death of his faithful servants.

Psalm 116:15

One of the hardest things in life is when one seemingly dies too young.

Perhaps you've heard of the story of Horatio Spafford.[1] He was a lawyer and businessman in Chicago, where he had extensive real estate holdings. He was known as a kind and generous man who supported various missions, including the YMCA and the Presbyterian Theological Seminary. Despite his successes, in October 1871, Spafford's real estate holdings, including his law office, were essentially wiped out by the infamous Chicago Fire.

Even though he was mired in debt, by November 1873 Spafford felt it necessary to get his wife Anna and four daughters (Annie, eleven; Margaret, nine; Elizabeth, five; and Tanetta, two) away from their dreary circumstances. They were to set sail for Europe aboard the *Ville du Havre*, a large ship well acquainted with the long Atlantic voyage. At the last minute, Horatio was delayed when an opportunity arose to sell some of his fire-stricken properties.

The voyage began on November 15, 1873. On November 22, the *Ville du Havre* was inexplicably struck by the *Loch Earn* at 2 a.m. The collision created a twelve-foot-deep hole in the *Ville*, and water came pouring in while despairing passengers clad only in nightgowns rushed to the deck. The ship sank within twelve minutes.

Only Anna survived. When she reached port, she sent a telegram to Horatio, telling him of their great loss: "Saved alone. What shall I do?" In dealing with their grief, both Anna and Horatio took to writing. It was Horatio, when reflecting upon the loss of his four daughters, who penned the now famous words:

> When peace, like a river, attendeth my way,
> When sorrows, like sea-billows roll
> Whatever my lot, Thou hast taught me to know
> It is well, it is well with my soul.

Spafford's hymn, now his legacy, has been sung in countless church services around the globe. Its words provide hope to those in trial and suffering. It's been a beacon of hope for many a mourner in funeral services far and wide. His loss became his legacy.

Spafford's story reminds us that in God's bigger picture, He is always using the bigger story to impact the world for His greater glory.

O Lord, thank You for Horatio Spafford's story. He suffered great loss, but You used his loss, which led to an incredible hymn providing comfort to so many people. Teach me how the trials and losses in my life might be used as well to minister to those who are suffering and hurting.

DAY 75

WE ARE PART *of a* GREAT STORY

> Therefore tell him I am making my covenant of peace with him. He and his descendants will have a covenant of a lasting priesthood, because he was zealous for the honor of his God and made atonement for the Israelites.
>
> Numbers 25:12–13

It's a powerful thing when God makes a covenant. When God makes a covenant with man, it's typically the kind of thing that changes the direction of families for generations.

In Numbers 25, God makes a covenant with Phinehas—a covenant of peace, and it's a covenant for a lasting priesthood. When I read those words, I'm amazed. I'd love that covenant for myself—a covenant of peace, to have a lasting and enduring priesthood. What's the story of Phinehas?

After leaving Egypt, the Israelites could have gone up to the promised land. Instead of acting in faith that God would give them the land, the Israelites acted in fear. They saw their opposition and said, "There's no way we can win!" Because they chose fear over faith, God sentenced them to forty years of wandering in the wilderness.

As they wandered in the wilderness, they intermarried and had adulterous relationships with the surrounding pagan tribes. These relationships impacted the people's hearts by turning them away from God. In a brazen incident, one of the Israelite men brought a foreigner into the camp, and Phinehas killed them. While his actions might seem harsh by today's standards, they represent zeal for God's holiness and the kind of attitude we ought to have toward our sin.

Here's what I love in God's economy. While God makes this promise in the book of Numbers to Phinehas, it might seem to go unrecognized. Quiet. Silent. Some might even say, "So what? What good is a covenant of peace?" Some four hundred years later, when King David was on his throne, he recognized Phinehas. He wrote a psalm that specifically mentioned him:

> But Phinehas stood up and intervened, and the plague was checked. This was credited to him as righteousness for endless generations to come. (Psalm 106:30–31)

God recognizes when we act in faith. He sees when we live a life of worship, and He's pleased by it. That's a big idea. God takes note of our obedience. So the simple question is: Where can you step out in your life today? Is there an area of correction that needs to be made in your life? Is there an area of correction in your surrounding world? Is there a place where you need to be bold in the name of Christ? The blessing of living in that way is for generations.

O Lord, I love the beauty of Your Word. May I step out in faith and zeal today in my life for the sake of Your holiness.

DAY 76

THE GREATEST MAN?

> Truly I tell you, among those born of women there has not risen anyone greater than John the Baptist.
>
> Matthew 11:11

When you think of people with great legacies, who does it make you think about? Perhaps it is those with big families? Big companies? A résumé of success?

I'm not sure we'd think of John the Baptist when we think of legacy. He was a single man. He never married. He never had children. He never traveled far from his place of birth. We actually have no record of his occupation. Somewhere around the age of thirty, he moved to the wilderness. Quite likely, his home was a cave. His possessions were few.

He dressed in clothes made of camel hair, and he had a leather belt around his waist. Camel hair clothing, by nature, would have been rough on the skin. It's

The Greatest Man?

the clothing of an ascetic—a monk dedicated to his ministry—and served as a reminder that life here on earth is temporary at best. We are not citizens of this planet. But the camel hair clothing was also a reference to a calling. John was to be the next Elijah, a prophet who dressed the same way (2 Kings 1:8). Ultimately, his clothing and way of life was also a reference to a life of faith—"They went about in sheepskins and goatskins, destitute, persecuted and mistreated" (Heb. 11:37).

He ate locusts and wild honey. He preached a message of repentance in the wilderness. He called the religious leaders of the day a brood of vipers. He even challenged the ruling elite, which led to his imprisonment and ultimate death.

His ministry proved to be short. When Jesus came, the crowds went away. Even his own disciples went to follow Jesus. And he was okay with that. He said that he only had one job: to be the voice of one calling in the wilderness and to prepare the way of the Lord (Isa. 40:3). When his own disciples questioned him about the loss of the crowds, the loss of his ministry, John replied simply:

> A person can receive only what is given them from heaven. You yourselves can testify that I said, "I am not the Messiah but am sent ahead of him." (John 3:27–28)

Against this backdrop, Jesus called John the Baptist the greatest among those born of women. A single man with a great legacy. What made John the Baptist so great? It might surprise you. John lived out what God asked him to do. He didn't get distracted. He just obeyed. Way to go, John! Whether single or married, rich or poor, we all can live a great legacy by being faithful with what God asks us to do.

O Lord, I pray that You would switch my thinking. Great legacies are not advertised on TV or social media. Great legacies start with lives of simple obedience—doing what You ask of us in this day and moment. Help me to be faithful in this day.

DAY 77

THE ORDINARY, EVERYDAY LEGACY

> These were all commended for their faith, yet none of them received what had been promised, since God had planned something better for us so that only together with us would they be made perfect.
>
> Hebrews 11:39–40

We live in a celebrity culture. How many follows, likes, and views on social media someone has may dictate their success. In some respects, it might be easy to view the Bible with the same celebrity mindset.

Think about it. There's father Abraham. Moses the great deliverer. David the warrior king. Daniel in the lion's den. Isaiah the prophet. Paul the great defender of the faith. Jesus the great Redeemer. When we consider those headlines, it might be easy to shrink back and think, "Well, I'm not great like that."

But God in His grace and mercy is good to remind us of the lesser stories—people who are never even named—who enter the narrative of Scripture for even the briefest of moments. They, too, are part of the grand narrative, the story, and the legacy of the greatest love story ever. Where to start?

Think about the shepherds in the field. They were a group of nameless outcasts, yet they were the first to see the angels and worship the newborn King. They were the first to share the news of the Messiah with the world. Or consider after Jesus was born and Mary and Joseph took Him to the temple. There was Simeon, a righteous and devout man. He entered the story just to say that he'd received a vision that he'd get to see the Messiah before he died. Or Anna the prophetess—she had only a few lines but affirmed that Jesus would bring the redemption of Israel. These three examples are found just within the Christmas story in Luke 2.

Or consider Ananias. In Acts 9, he was told to go and restore Paul's eyesight. Ananias was understandably afraid since Paul had murdered Christians. But Ananias obeyed and was part of the launch of Paul's ministry. If you continue through the book of Acts, there are countless other no-names. In Acts 2, there was the first group of believers who responded to Peter's sermon.

The Ordinary, Everyday Legacy

In Acts 4:34–35, there were those who made the work of ministry possible by selling land and houses to fund the ministry. In Acts 12:12, there were many gathered to pray for the church and for Peter's release from prison.

Think about the churches that were planted during Paul's missionary journeys. Groups of believers in Corinth, Ephesus, Thessalonica, Berea, Philippi, Galatia—it's hard to say how many churches Paul planted. But think about each and every one of those churches filled with believers in Jesus Christ who advanced the gospel. They are part of a grand narrative. They are part of a great legacy.

O Lord, forgive me for thinking that it is only the stage that matters. Your kingdom is about those who live faithfully every day in the communities they are planted in.

DAY 78

MARY'S MAGNIFICAT

> From now on all generations will call me blessed, for the Mighty One has done great things for me—holy is his name.
>
> Luke 1:48–49

In the moment, things couldn't seem much worse. She was a teenager, pregnant, pledged to be married (which was as good as married), and her husband Joseph, a good and decent man, was considering a divorce. A divorce meant she could be stoned or just shamed the rest of her life. You can imagine that her parents weren't happy and her neighbors weren't happy—she'd always been a good girl, and now *this*.

But Mary saw things differently. An angel appeared to her. The angel said that she was favored by God. She would conceive by the Holy Spirit and give birth to the Messiah. This Messiah would reign over Jacob and his descendants, and his kingdom would never end. Mary believed the angel.

Put yourself in Mary's shoes. What would you believe? Considering your current reality—pregnant, a doubting husband—it would be pretty hard to believe you conceived by the Holy Spirit! To be found unfaithful, at worst, meant death by stoning. But at least stoning would be quick compared to the hushed whispers, the conversations that wouldn't include her anymore, and the shame her situation would bring to her parents and her relatives.

Mary didn't stay there. Her response to the angel was, in essence, "Let's roll!" What allowed Mary to have that kind of response? Mary didn't just get caught up in the moment, the trouble of the day. Mary had a generational perspective.

She had a generational perspective of the past. In her Magnificat, she looks to what God has done in the past:

> He has performed mighty deeds with his arm; he has scattered those who are proud in their inmost thoughts. He has brought down rulers from their thrones but has lifted up the humble. He has filled the hungry with good things but has sent the rich away empty. (Luke 1:51–53)

But Mary also looks forward. She knows the significance of what is occurring and the implications for the future:

> From now on all generations will call me blessed, for the Mighty One has done great things for me—holy is his name. His mercy extends to those who fear him, from generation to generation. (Luke 1:48–50)

It's this view—of generations past and generations to come—that allows Mary to endure the present moment of shame from friends and family. She knows that God has done good things in the past and He'll do good things in the future.

O Lord, allow me to see my present circumstances in view of Your generational work in the past and the work that You'll do in the future. How I praise You for this work!

DAY 79

HE REMEMBERED WHERE HOME WAS

> So Joseph also went up from the town of Nazareth in Galilee to Judea, to Bethlehem the town of David, because he belonged to the house and line of David.
>
> Luke 2:4

As I've mentioned in previous devotions, my family moved frequently when I was growing up because our church denomination required pastors to move every two years. I was born in Emporia, Kansas, but spent time in parts of New Mexico, parts of Texas, and parts of Oklahoma. I went to twelve or thirteen different schools over those years. For much of that time, I felt like I was a nomad with no sense of belonging. It wasn't until moving to Oklahoma that I finally felt like we had a home.

I know many people have that same experience and never feel like they fully belong. Some of them are military. Some may be missionary kids. Some may be disconnected from their parents. There may be lots of reasons for that disconnect. But that disconnect is not uncommon. There's a surprising number of people today who don't know the names of their grandparents, let alone their great-grandparents. Great-great-grandparents are completely out of the question.

That's why I'm so impressed with the story of Joseph. The Bible very simply states that Joseph went up from Nazareth to Bethlehem "because he belonged to the house and line of David" (Luke 2:4). Joseph knew where home was.

In Matthew 1:17, we are told, "Thus there were fourteen generations in all from Abraham to David, fourteen from David to the exile to Babylon, and fourteen from the exile to the Messiah." It had been at least 840 years since Abraham and his descendants first traipsed to the promised land.

You could argue that Joseph's family lineage was questionable. Even King David—there was a lot of trouble there. Rape, murder, estrangement, conspiracies against the throne, competition for the throne—they were all part of David's rule. And in the generations that followed King David, there were only a few faithful kings. Many in Joseph's family line were evil, unfaithful, and forgettable. It would have been easy for subsequent generations not to talk about their family heritage.

Not Joseph. He knew the family stories, and they pointed him home to Bethlehem.

I love this idea. In our families, we take the good and the bad. We celebrate the good. We learn from the bad. We take the entire story. It's our fabric. Our tapestry. Our stories are what make us whole, what make us family.

O Lord, thank You for reminding me of Joseph. Through hundreds of years and hundreds of ancestors, some good and some bad, Joseph still remembered where his home was. Help me to remember my roots and to embrace my entire story, the entire fabric. I admit that I may need to confront some parts of my story that I've avoided, but let me do so with courage.

DAY 80

IT'S NEVER TOO LATE

> Jephthah the Gileadite was a mighty warrior. His father was Gilead; his mother was a prostitute.
>
> Judges 11:1

About six to eight times a year, our family hosts leaders and their spouses at Hobby Lobby to share some of our family's journey. Before we begin our time together, I'm always careful to share my disclaimers with the group.

One of those disclaimers is that our story is not your story. What I mean by that statement is that what God has called our family to do may not be the same as what He calls another family to do. For instance, in this time and season, God has called us to give 50 percent of our profit. But He may not call everyone to do that.

Sometimes during these gatherings, I'll also have families come up to me and say, "It's too late for our family. The toothpaste is already out of the tube."

There's not always the chance or the opportunity to go deep with those stories, but I always try to tell them that it's never too late. There's always an opportunity for change.

That's why I love the story of Jephthah. He didn't have the best beginning. In Judges 11:1, we are told that he was the son of a prostitute. His father, Gilead, had other legitimate sons by his wife. I'm not sure what happened or why—perhaps it was jealousy—but when those sons grew up, they told Jephthah he would not share in *their* inheritance. They literally drove him out of the house; he had to flee into the wilderness.

You can imagine the emotional devastation Jephthah faced. Driven from his father, driven from his family, driven from any inheritance, he lived in the wilderness where the Bible says worthless fellows gathered around him. For Jephthah, he could have remained stuck in misery, thinking, *It's too late for me.*

But God always has a way of redeeming and turning the story around in ways we cannot see or imagine.

So it was with Jephthah. An enemy tribe gathered for war against Israel. Recognizing that they didn't have the right person to lead them into battle, the elders of Gilead went to Jephthah in the wilderness. They asked Jephthah to become the leader of their entire tribe.

At first he was skeptical of the people who previously rejected him, but eventually he agreed to their request.

I hope you don't miss the message. God took Jephthah's rejection from his own family and turned it into something much bigger and something much better. It just took time and patience.

O Lord, thank You for reminding me that, even though my legacy may seem broken, You can restore and redeem because that is Your very nature.

DAY 81

IT WASN'T SUPPOSED *to* BE THIS WAY

> Then Naomi said to her two daughters-in-law, "Go back, each of you, to your mother's home. May the LORD show you kindness, as you have shown kindness to your dead husbands and to me. May the LORD grant that each of you will find rest in the home of another husband."
>
> Ruth 1:8–9

What do you cling to when all seems lost?

We can imagine the storyline. A new family moved into the neighborhood. They were foreigners, and in the past their tribes clashed. But this family seemed different. For one thing, they had two handsome sons. Before you knew it, Ruth and Orpah found themselves married to those handsome sons.

They were quickly welcomed into the family. In addition to her new husband, Ruth loved her new mother-in-law, Naomi. Naomi's singular faith in God was unique and different. But the honeymoon didn't last long. Tragedy struck. First, Naomi's husband died, and then her two sons died. Ruth's husband was gone, and with him her dreams of family, of children, of legacy.

When Naomi made the decision to return to her homeland, Ruth was faced with a decision. She could return to the comfort of the home she had grown up in, or she could face the unknown and travel to a land where she knew no one other than her mother-in-law. Naomi told her to stay. She'd have better prospects for a husband if she stayed. Naomi could promise her nothing if Ruth came with her.

Despite Naomi's insistence, Ruth made this famous appeal:

> Don't urge me to leave you or to turn back from you. Where you go I will go, and where you stay I will stay. Your people will be my people and your God my God. Where you die I will die, and there I will be buried. May the LORD deal with me, be it ever so severely, if even death separates you and me. (Ruth 1:16–17)

She was intrigued by Naomi's faith. It was enough to cling to when everything else seemed broken. In returning to her homeland, Naomi found a Redeemer. Ruth married and bore a child who became part of God's overall redemption story.

God, in His wonderful way, redeems the broken. He takes the hopeless story and turns it hopeful. He takes the lonely story and fills it with family.

O Lord, thank You for reminding me that, even when everything seems hopeless, if I cling to faith, You will redeem and restore.

DAY 82

WRITE YOUR OBITUARY

> It gave me great joy when some believers came and testified about your faithfulness to the truth, telling how you continue to walk in it.
>
> 3 John 3

We write our obituaries while we are living. Some people take that exercise to heart, and they literally write out their obituary. But what I mean is that we live the story we want others to tell about us someday. What do you want your family to say about you? What about your friends? Your coworkers? What will people say about your character? What will they list as your greatest gifts? Will they call you generous or greedy? What will be your greatest acts of service?

Sometimes the Scriptures speak to us in that way. There are people who flit across the pages for just a brief moment. The book of 3 John is like that. It's a book of

Write Your Obituary

just fifteen verses, and those verses primarily reference two characters: Gaius and Diotrephes. As John wrote, he might as well have been writing the obituaries of each.

What do we learn about Gaius? John had heard reports about Gaius from fellow believers. He was faithful to the truth. He walked in it. How do we know? Gaius served his fellow brothers and sisters in Christ—even those who were strangers to him (v. 5). His hospitality and his love were well known (v. 6). Gaius invited them in and then sent them out more encouraged. In all of it, his life honored God. That's a great testimony!

John's obituary about Diotrephes is troubling. He thought of himself first. He did not welcome John (v. 9). But it got worse. He spread "malicious nonsense" (v. 10). He was a mean gossip. He did not practice hospitality. To the contrary, he prevented others from practicing hospitality and sought to put them out of the church (v. 10).

We don't know much about these characters other than the words written here. There's little question that Gaius was a guy we'd like to meet. In fact, he'd welcome us, love us, serve us, and encourage us. But Diotrephes was another story. He sounds like a mean, ill-tempered man. He thought of himself first—not others. He didn't welcome others. He was the Scrooge of the Bible.

It's a bit sobering to think that the obituaries of Gaius and Diotrephes are written down here in the Bible. The testimony of their lives has been on public display for generations of Bible readers. Maybe that's a bit of sobering up that we all need: to think that all of our lives are on public display to be revealed on that day in heaven when our lives will be judged before the judgment seat of Christ (2 Cor. 5:10).

We all ought to give some thought to the obituaries we are writing. Lives of faithfulness, love, hospitality, and generosity will always yield a good testimony. Lives of greed, selfishness, and division will never yield a good report.

O Lord, remind me again that my life is not hidden. You see all. Help me then to live a life of love and faithfulness before You and to write a good obituary.

DAY 83

A SINGLE PERSON'S LEGACY

> You must not marry and have sons or daughters in this place.
>
> Jeremiah 16:2

During the CEO and leadership events we host, from time to time I'll have someone come up to me and ask, "I'm single. Can I have a legacy?"

Legacy is not just for those who are married and have children. While it might be easy to lift up marriage as the ideal, I think it's interesting to note the number of single people in the Bible.

- Jeremiah the prophet was specifically told not to marry. In fact, in the same chapter, Jeremiah is told to not go to funerals or weddings. He was not to engage in so many of the ceremonies that make up life in community. Yet there's little doubt that Jeremiah had an incredible impact on the nation of Israel.

- The apostle Paul said in 1 Corinthians 7:32 that it is a good thing to remain unmarried because the single person can be focused upon the Lord's affairs. Paul described singleness as the better state (v. 38).
- John the Baptist was the prophet in the wilderness. His simple lifestyle would not have been a great match for a family. But his legacy is unquestioned. Jesus Himself said that there was no one greater born among women than John (Matt. 11:11).
- In Luke 2, Anna the prophetess was married just seven years before becoming a widow. The bulk of her life was spent as a single widow. Yet she witnessed to Mary and Joseph of the divinity of Jesus.
- In Acts 16, Lydia stands out. In a day when women were linked to their husbands, Lydia stands alone as a merchant of purple cloth. After she came to faith, she asked Paul to baptize her entire household.

A Single Person's Legacy

Perhaps most importantly, each of us is called as an individual to have our own legacy. Second Corinthians 5:10 says, "Each of us may receive what is due us for the things done while in the body, whether good or bad." We are accountable as individuals, not as a family.

A single person has the same opportunity to impact generations through the manner of their life, witness to others, and discipleship of men and women. Indeed, the single person can directly impact whose names are written in the Book of Life. That kind of impact is the greatest legacy a person can ask for.

O Lord, thank You for reminding me that every person has a legacy—whether single or married. The legacy of the single person is just as important as that of the married person. Let me be an encouragement to all to be part of lasting spiritual legacies.

DAY 84

QUESTIONING YOUR LEGACY

> When John, who was in prison, heard about the deeds of the Messiah, he sent his disciples to ask him, "Are you the one who is to come, or should we expect someone else?"
>
> Matthew 11:2–3

He'd labored hard. The expectations started young. His parents always told him that he'd be the one to prepare the way for the Messiah. The Messiah—the long-awaited Messiah! He was the next Elijah. Not exactly small shoes to fill.

Then finally the day came. It was time to start. He moved to the wilderness. A cave. He learned to eat meagerly. Locusts. Some honey. His clothing was simple. A rough tunic made of camel hair. He didn't mind the spartan lifestyle. He'd never really fit in; his eyes were wild with life.

Questioning Your Legacy

But boy, did he have a voice. He could speak over the waters, and the sound carried. He spoke with the same fire as the light in his eyes. It had been a long time since the people of Israel had heard such a message. When they heard him speak, they thought about the legends of Jeremiah, Isaiah, and Daniel.

His message was difficult. He spoke of the people's hardness of heart, their need for repentance because the kingdom of God was at hand. Many responded. Many were baptized. And one day, the Messiah, Jesus, did come. He came out to see John and asked to be baptized by his very hand. What a great day!

And then, just like that, it was over. Slowly, the crowds died away. Even his own disciples began to follow Jesus, as they should. The contrarian in John took over, and he challenged King Herod on the legality of his marriage. That challenge led to John's imprisonment.

There he sat, contemplating his fate. Would he live? Would he die at the hand of the king? Meanwhile, the legend of Jesus grew. John heard the stories of the healings, the miracles, and the lives changed. But as he sat in the confines of the prison, he also heard the criticism. Who was Jesus? A challenger to Herod? A pretender? Would He bring peace to Israel?

John fretted. As the differing stories evolved, he wondered if he'd wasted his days, so he sent his disciples to Jesus. "Are you really the one we've been waiting for?" Jesus was quick to respond with a yes—"The blind receive sight, the lame walk, those who have leprosy are cleansed, the deaf hear, the dead are raised, and the good news is proclaimed to the poor" (Matt. 11:5).

Don't despair, dear reader. If you question your legacy, what you've given your life to, your doubt is normal. Like John, entrust the results of your life and legacy to Jesus. He's the one responsible for the outcomes.

O Lord, I love this reminder that even the great prophets had their doubts. I entrust my life and legacy to You.

DAY 85

HE DIED TOO YOUNG?

And they overcame him by the blood of the Lamb and by the word of their testimony, and they did not love their lives to the death.

Revelation 12:11 NKJV

He died at twenty-eight years of age. He was still healthy, vibrant, intelligent; he'd been married just over two years; their daughter was just ten months old. By all accounts, it was a sad story. Some call it a wasted life.[1]

His name? Jim Elliot. He was born in 1927 in Portland, Oregon. He grew up in a family of faith, and his entire life was projected toward sharing the gospel. He attended Wheaton College with the idea that it would prepare him for world missions. But for him it was not just any mission—it had to be something hard. A people group that no one had reached. A journal entry from this period describes his singular devotion:

> He is no fool who gives what he cannot keep to gain what he cannot lose.[2]

Elliot and a group of friends ultimately settled upon taking the gospel to the Huaorani people, then known as the Aucas, a fierce tribe deep in the jungles of Ecuador.

In 1952, Elliot traveled to Ecuador and began learning Spanish and some of the culture. In October 1953, he married Elisabeth Howard, and in February 1955, their daughter, Valerie, was born. By the fall of that year, Elliot and a small team working with him began to make an initial outreach with the Huaorani.

Their first contact with the Huaorani proved friendly. But on January 8, 1956, the Huaorani returned to the missionary camp and attacked. Elliot and his friends were all killed.

Some might say that Jim Elliot's missionary efforts were a waste. He never got to share the gospel with a people so needy for it. But the story didn't end with his death. Two years after his death, his wife Elisabeth and the sister of one of his slain friends took the gospel to the Huaorani. Many became believers, and the tribe is a peaceful one today.

Elliot's journal was discovered during the recovery of the bodies. His final journal entry reads:

Perhaps in mercy he shall give me a host of children [i.e., converts] that I may lead them through the vast star fields to explore his delicacies whose finger ends set them to burning. But if not, if only I may see him, touch his garments, and smile into his eyes—ah then, not stars nor children shall matter, only himself.[3]

There is no better illustration of the idea that legacy is what we set in motion than Elliot's life.

O Lord, may I live with a zeal toward You that is singular, pointing only to You and setting aflame those around me with the same zeal.

DAY 86

THE LUMBER LEGACY

> For the LORD takes delight in his people; he crowns the humble with victory. Let his faithful people rejoice in this honor and sing for joy on their beds.
>
> Psalm 149:4–5

There are so many great legacy stories. I could write another book of them. But one that I wanted to make sure to include is the story of the accidental lumberman.

On December 17, 1850, Robert Alexander Long was born in Shelbyville, Kentucky.[1] He was one of nine children. He grew up working on his father's farm and had a deep faith. By the age of twenty-two, Robert was ready to try his hand at business. He moved to Kansas City with $700—his share of the farm profits. With his savings dwindling, he started a hay business and cut tons of hay. He also bought lumber and built sheds to store the hay.

The hay business failed, but he learned that he could sell the lumber from the sheds for more than the hay. A lumber business was born. At first, Long ordered lumber and sold it, but eventually the business grew to a full-scale lumberyard. Later, he expanded to lumber mills and raw timber. By the early 1900s, Long's business included ten sawmill plants with timber land in Texas, Arkansas, and Louisiana.[2] By 1906, Long's lumber business was the largest in the world.

But Long's business was far from his only influence. His strong faith motivated him to provide good living conditions for his employees. An entire town was built around the lumber operations in the state of Washington and was appropriately called Longview. He invested generously in his hometown of Kansas City, Missouri. There, he gave to causes like the city's first public library, the YMCA, the first high school, a train station, and a hotel for visitors to Kansas City. These gifts came in addition to his own giving to his local church.

When it came time to establish a monument for those who fought during World War I, the city leaders turned to Long to lead the capital campaign. In just ten days they collected $2.5 million dollars.[3] Today, because of Long's leadership, the Liberty Memorial stands as a beacon and tribute over the city.

Long died in 1934. As the lumber industry suffered a downturn, so did Long's fortunes. At his death, his company had to file for bankruptcy reorganization. Some said his financial fortunes suffered in light of his extravagant generosity. But today in Kansas City, there are colleges and parks named after this man, whose legacy became a great force in not just Kansas City but other cities as well.

Long's influence is a remarkable testimony of one man deeply committed to a legacy of faith and generosity. My prayer is that we might see another generation of people like Robert Alexander Long, people committed to the good of a city.

O Lord, thank You for humble people of the past like Robert Long. Would You raise up an entire generation of people who would follow suit to influence their own communities with a legacy of faith and generosity?

DAY 87

MY BROKEN LEGACY

> Moses said to God, "Suppose I go to the Israelites and say to them, 'The God of your fathers has sent me to you,' and they ask me, 'What is his name?' Then what shall I tell them?"
>
> Exodus 3:13

Have you ever gotten to a place where you said, "My story is broken. My legacy is messed up"? I have. By 1985, everything I'd touched had been successful. I'd risen through the ranks of store management with promotion after promotion and then started my business, and it all seemed to be going great. But in 1985, everything came crashing down, and the bank wrote me a letter saying they were going to foreclose on us.

I felt like such a failure. My kids and in-laws worked for me. Hundreds of employees depended on me. I could see the loss of it all. It was embarrassing. I didn't know what to do or where to go. All I could do was pray.

I suspect Moses was like that. He'd been adopted into the court of the pharaoh. There, he experienced abundance—plenty of food and drink. Life was good and comfortable. But Moses knew where he came from, and every day he saw his own people, the children of Israel, mistreated, beaten, and struck down by the very people whose palace he inhabited. He couldn't reconcile these two worlds.

One day, he saw an Egyptian mistreating one of his people. Rage spread through him, and in that anger, he struck the man. Murder. He buried his misdeed in the sands of Egypt. But misdeeds never stay buried—someone saw his act of violence. Word filtered out to Pharaoh and to his own people. Moses was a wanted man. He fled.

There in the wilderness, Moses tended sheep. A far cry from the courts of Pharaoh. Sometimes under a starry sky or in a quiet moment as the wind stirred him, Moses remembered. It was a dream that haunted him. And over and over again, he remembered feeling the hatred rising in his heart and the raising of his hand. The dead body at his feet. His shameful, feeble attempts at a cover-up. The memories lingered.

For forty years, he toiled in the desert. His legacy was broken. God could surely never use him, until one day he saw a strange sight: a burning bush not consumed. Amazingly, the God of his fathers, the great Yahweh, called out to him, called him by name. He told Moses that He wanted to use *him* to deliver his people out of slavery.

Is it any wonder that Moses asks, in essence, "Why would anyone believe me?" But that's the way God is. He takes those with even a seemingly broken legacy, and He says, "I still want to use you for good and for greatness!"

O Lord, thank You for reminding us through this story of Moses that there is no broken legacy. Like Moses, I come with humility, and I offer my life and say to You, "Use me as You wish for Your kingdom's sake."

DAY 88

THE MUSICIAN'S LEGACY

> These are the men David put in charge of the music in the house of the LORD. . . . Asaph, who served at his right hand: Asaph son of Berekiah, the son of Shimea.
>
> 1 Chronicles 6:31, 39

There are a lot of stories of families and individuals who don't succeed. Probably more than we care to remember. But what about the good stories?

I'd like to tell you a good story. It's the story of Asaph. When King Saul was the king of Israel, things were a mess. Saul was a paranoid, suspicious leader. Everyone under his leadership walked on eggshells, including his own son. When Saul died in battle and the kingdom was placed in David's hand, a new day, a breath of fresh air, arrived.

The Musician's Legacy

King David instituted vast and sweeping reforms. God was placed in the center; worship and adoration occupied a primary spot. To elevate worship, David wrote psalms and hymns. In 1 Chronicles 6, David appointed a worship team.

One of those team members was Asaph. He was probably just a teenager when he was first appointed. His brother was appointed to the same team. But as Asaph's career developed, he became the chief musician (1 Chron. 16:5). As he grew and improved, he became a psalm writer as well. In fact, there are twelve specific psalms (50, 73–83) that were written by Asaph and reflected his big view of God in the face of evil.

But Asaph's influence wasn't limited to David's time. His service continued into Solomon's court.

Fast-forward one hundred years later, and one of the sons of Asaph provided a prophetic word of protection during the time of King Jehoshaphat (2 Chron. 20:14). During Hezekiah's reign 140 years later, the sons of Asaph were asked to cleanse and consecrate the temple. Another eighty years later, as King Josiah sought to turn Israel back to God, he asked a son of Asaph to be part of the worship (2 Chron. 35:15). Still another four hundred years later, Ezra recorded that there were 148 sons of Asaph who returned from exile. They were part of laying the foundation of the temple and rebuilding the wall around Jerusalem.

One family. Hundreds of years of pointing people to worship. What a vision for one family's life. I imagine that someday in heaven we'll meet many sons of Asaph.

I love that vision for my life and for everyone reading this book. I pray that there will be many sons and daughters—generations of them—that we'll meet in heaven.

O Lord, thanks for this encouraging word from the family of Asaph. I pray this blessing over my life and the life of my family, that there will be many in heaven as the result of my life and our family.

DAY 89
CULTURAL LEGACIES

> Tell it to your children, and let your children tell it to their children, and their children to the next generation.
>
> Joel 1:3

Deep in the mountains of Pakistan, near the border of Afghanistan, there is a group of people known as the Kalash.[1] There are roughly three thousand of them. They are surrounded on all sides by Muslim tribes—some of them hostile to the Kalash.

Some think the origins of the people rest with Alexander the Great, who left behind some of his bloodline after invading. Compared to the neighboring tribes, the Kalash are distinctly Caucasian with fair complexions and many of them with blue eyes, and they wear bright and colorful clothing. They are not Muslim—instead, they worship many gods and follow a mix of Hinduism and animism, believing that everything in nature has a spiritual element.

They have their own unique religious practices, including festivals and dances that they've handed down from generation to generation. Despite being surrounded by a distinctly Muslim world, they maintain the Kalash culture. Only recently, when a tunnel was constructed, allowing for road traffic, have they seen more and more challenges to maintaining their culture.

The Kalash represent the idea of a cultural legacy. When one family comes together and teaches a particular way of life, and then their children have children and teach the same way of life, you have the beginning of a cultural legacy. That cultural legacy has a powerful hold. It serves as a way of preventing the melting into the surrounding culture, as the Kalash demonstrate. It likewise serves as a point of attraction for others who aren't part of that culture.

That way of life—the traditions, the festivals, the songs, the dress, the language, the practices—tells us that not only are we different from the surrounding groups but that we are also part of something we can draw our identity from.

So it is with God's design. He desires that we build cultural legacies. That is the premise of Joel 1:3. Tell your children. Let your children tell their children. And their children the next generation. Tell them that the

Lord our God is one. He alone is to be served, and He wants us to love Him and to love others. We live by a different set of values. Jesus said it a bit differently: "By this everyone will know that you are my disciples, if you love one another" (John 13:35).

From the very beginning, this was God's simple design—perpetuating lasting cultural legacies. We see families like the Kalash people still working and preserving. Will you undertake the challenge of your own cultural legacy?

O Lord, thank You for this challenge to build a cultural legacy in and through my own family and thus perpetuate Your name throughout the world and through the generations.

DAY 90

FINALLY HOME

And I heard a loud voice from the throne saying, "Look! God's dwelling place is now among the people, and he will dwell with them. They will be his people, and God himself will be with them and be their God."

Revelation 21:3

We spend our lives wishing for places and seasons we are not in. When we were young, we wished for summer vacation from school. Of course, by the end of summer, we wished for the start of school so we could have something to do. When we start our working years, we wish for things like getting married, establishing our careers, starting a family, or getting a house. When we have kids, we wish they would get out of diapers or stop nursing, and later we wish for graduation, college, and some level of independence.

Always rushing. Always wishing. All the while, in all our rushing, we give plenty of thought to what we will eat, drink, or wear, but we give so little thought to heaven. Funny, isn't it—the very place we'll spend all of eternity, and we give it so little thought.

Sometimes when I think of heaven, I compare it to how Barbara and I will go on a long trip. It's always a lot more work than you think to prepare, stuffing things in the suitcase, making sure you don't forget anything. It's all the little details—grabbing your driver's license, downloading your boarding pass, finding a parking spot, getting through security, and then waiting and more waiting. There's always an extra rush of anxiety when we travel. Yet it's all great fun to be away, to explore and find new places.

But when it's time to leave, I wonder how there seems to be less room in my suitcase on the way back, and we experience the same rush of activity—getting directions in an unfamiliar place, getting a rental car returned, and finally boarding the plane home.

There's a weariness when we land, when we finally collect our bags, and we settle into a musty car for the drive home. We pull into our driveway, flip the garage door switch, and collect all the bags so we only have to make one trip. As we stumble through the doorway, dropping our bags, we say, "Finally, finally home."

It takes a bit to unwind, but Barbara and I will sit there at our kitchen table, looking out over the landscape. Conversing. Comfortable. Maybe sipping on a lemonade.

But on that day, it won't be Barbara. It will be Jesus, and He'll look at me with a look of gladness, a look of satisfaction. And strongly, confidently, He'll say to me, "You are finally, finally home!"

O Lord, would You stir my imagination through Your Holy Spirit and Your Word and give me a better picture of what heaven's going to be like?

Notes

Day 6 Eternity in Our Hearts
1. "About Nicky Cruz, Christian Evangelist & Best-Selling Author," *Nicky Cruz Outreach*, accessed April 16, 2024, https://nickycruz.org/about-2/.

Day 9 Keep the Shoreline in Mind
1. Stephen R. Covey, *The 7 Habits of Highly Effective People: Powerful Lessons in Personal Change* (Fireside, 1989), 98.
2. "Florence Chadwick," Encyclopedia.com, updated September 11, 2024, https://www.encyclopedia.com/people/sports-and-games/sports-biographies/florence-may-chadwick.

Day 24 There Is Accountability
1. Troy Segal, "Enron Scandal and Accounting Fraud: What Happened?," Investopedia, updated June 3, 2024, https://www.investopedia.com/updates/enron-scandal-summary.

Day 25 There Is Reward and Loss
1. Peter Bondarenko, "Enron Scandal," *Britannica*, updated July 29, 2024, https://www.britannica.com/event/Enron-scandal.

Day 36 Eliminate the "And"

1. A. W. Tozer, *The Pursuit of God* (Christian Publications, 1993), 18.

Day 44 Life on Mission

1. Alessio Bresciani, "51 Mission Statement Examples from the World's Best Companies," *Alessio Bresciani* (blog), accessed April 17, 2024, https://alessiobresciani.com/foresight-strategy/51-mission-statement-examples-from-the-worlds-best-companies/.

Day 46 The Power of Celebration

1. Jesse Blackman and Susha Roberts, "7 Feasts That Point to Christ," Wycliffe Bible Translators, accessed April 17, 2024, https://www.wycliffe.org/feast/7-feasts-that-point-to-christ.

Day 52 What's Your Conduct Code?

1. Craig Impelman, "John Wooden's 7-Point Creed: 'Be True to Yourself,'" The Wooden Effect, December 13, 2016, https://www.thewoodeneffect.com/john-woodens-7-point-creed-true.

Day 53 The Freedom of Stewardship

1. Tozer, *Pursuit*, 27.

Day 54 The Importance of Discipline

1. *Merriam-Webster Dictionary*, "discipline," accessed April 17, 2024, https://www.merriam-webster.com/dictionary/discipline.

Day 57 Know Your Story

1. "New Survey from Ancestry Shows More than Half of Americans Can't Name All Four Grandparents," *Ancestry*, March 30, 2022, https://www.ancestry.com/corporate/newsroom/press-releases/new-survey-ancestry-shows-more-half-americans-cant-name-all-four.

Day 63 Fourteen Hundred Years of Family

1. Irene Herrera, "Building on Tradition—1,400 Years of a Family Business," *Works That Work*, no. 3, accessed April 17, 2024, https://worksthatwork.com/3/kongo-gumi.

Day 64 For a Thousand Generations

1. William T. O'Hara et al., "The World's Oldest Family Companies," *Family Business*, accessed April 15, 2024, https://www.griequity.com/resources/industryandissues/familybusiness/oldestinworld.html.

Day 65 Son of a Cymbal Maker

1. Lara Pellegrinelli, "A Family's 400-Year-Old Musical Secret Still Rings True," *New York Times*, August 3, 2018, https://www.nytimes.com/2018/08/03/arts/music/zildjian-cymbals-400-years.html.

2. "Celebrating 400 years of Zildjian Cymbals," Sweetwater, June 1, 2023, https://www.sweetwater.com/insync/zildjian-cymbals-history; Josh Merhar, "The Zildjian Company: 400 years in the Making," Boston Drum Lessons, December 6, 2019, https://www.bostondrumlessons.com/bostondrumlessonsblog/2019/12/2/the-zildjian-company-nearly-400-years-in-the-making.

Day 66 The Surprising Pastor's Legacy

1. Thomas A. Schafer, "Jonathan Edwards," *Britannica*, updated September 17, 2024, https://www.britannica.com/biography/Jonathan-Edwards.

2. A. E. Winship, *Jukes-Edwards: A Study in Education and Heredity* (R.L. Myers & Co, 1900), 14.

Day 67 The Janitor's Legacy

1. Travis Loller, "Funeral Held for Custodian Killed in Nashville Attack," *Associated Press*, April 4, 2023, https://www

.pressdemocrat.com/article/news/funeral-held-for-custodian-killed-in-nashville-attack.

2. Alisha Ebrahimji et al., "Young Children, a Substitute Teacher, the Head of Their School and Its Custodian. These Are the Victims of the Nashville School Shooting," *CNN*, March 31, 2023, https://www.cnn.com/2023/03/28/us/victims-covenant-school-shooting-nashville/index.html.

Day 70 The Loss of the World's Greatest Fortune

1. "How the Vanderbilt Family Lost Their Fortune," Dividend Real Estate, accessed April 16, 2024, https://dividendrealestate.com/vanderbilt.

2. Natalie Robehmed, "The Vanderbilts: How American Royalty Lost Their Crown Jewels," *Forbes*, updated June 17, 2019, https://www.forbes.com/sites/natalierobehmed/2014/07/14/the-vanderbilts-how-american-royalty-lost-their-crown-jewels/.

Day 71 The Rothschild Legacy

1. Jean Bouvier, "Rothschild Family," *Britannica*, updated August 18, 2024, https://www.britannica.com/topic/Rothschild-family; "History," Rothschild Foundation, accessed April 17, 2024, https://rothschildfoundation.eu/who-we-are/history.

Day 72 What Are Your Dying Wishes?

1. Niall Ferguson, *The House of Rothschild: Money's Prophets 1798–1848* (Penguin Books, 1998), 78.

2. Ferguson, *House of Rothschild*, 78.

Day 73 Sometimes You'll Never Know

1. Hugh Whelchel, "The Magi and the Eternal Effect of Our Work," The Gospel Coalition, December 13, 2013, https://www.thegospelcoalition.org/article/the-magi-and-the-eternal-effect-of-our-work/.

Day 74 Legacy Through Loss

1. Chris Fenner and Chuck Bumgardner, "It Is Well with My Soul with Ville du Havre," Hymnology Archive, updated July 15, 2021, https://www.hymnologyarchive.com/it-is-well-with-my-soul.

Day 85 He Died Too Young?

1. "Ode to Elisabeth Elliot," Sacred Story Ministries, accessed April 17, 2024, https://sacredstoryministries.org/ode-to-elisabeth-elliot.

2. Justin Taylor, "They Were No Fools: The Martyrdom of Jim Elliot and Four Other Missionaries," The Gospel Coalition, January 8, 2016, https://www.thegospelcoalition.org/blogs/justin-taylor/they-were-no-fools-60-years-ago-today-the-martyrdom-of-jim-elliot-and-four-other-missionaries/.

3. Tim Chester, "Jim Elliott Was No Fool," Crossway, January 8, 2018, https://www.crossway.org/articles/jim-elliot-was-no-fool.

Day 86 The Lumber Legacy

1. Rita Nell Patejdl, "Long's Legacy," R.A. Long Historical Society, accessed April 17, 2024, http://www.ralonghistoricalsociety.org.

2. Kathy Alexander, "Robert A. Long—Lumber Baron," Legends of America, updated May 2024, https://www.legendsofamerica.com/robert-long-lumber-baron/.

3. "Built by Kansas Citians, Embraced by the Nation," National WWI Museum and Memorial, accessed April 17, 2024, https://www.theworldwar.org/explore/our-story.

Day 89 Cultural Legacies

1. Joan Riera, "The Kalash People of Pakistan, the Last Animists of the Hindu Kush," Last Places, accessed April 17, 2024, https://lastplaces.com/en/travel-is-knowledge/kalash-people-pakistan.

DAVID GREEN borrowed $600 in 1970 to start making picture frames in a garage. He is now CEO of Hobby Lobby, which employs fifty thousand people at almost one thousand stores in forty-eight states and grosses $8 billion a year. The coauthor of *Giving It All Away . . . and Getting It All Back Again*, Green received the World Changer Award in 2013 and is a past recipient of the Ernst & Young Entrepreneur of the Year Award. David and his wife, Barbara, are the proud parents of three, grandparents of ten, and great-grandparents of seventeen (and counting). They live in Oklahoma City.

BILL HIGH is the CEO of Legacy Stone, a nonprofit ministry whose aim is to "raise family foundations for generational impact." The three themes for Bill's life are family, legacy, and generosity. After practicing law for twelve years, he moved into the charitable foundation world, where he began working with families. That work led to consulting work with families on crafting their plans for multigenerational legacies. He's worked with families in the United States and internationally. He's the author or coauthor of multiple books. He's married to his sweetheart, Brooke, and they have four children and four grandchildren. He can be found at BillHigh.com or LegacyStone.com.